THE OXFORD
MINI HISTORY
OF
BRITAIN

VOLUME II

THE OXFORD
MINI HISTORY OF BRITAIN

This five-volume series, edited by Kenneth O. Morgan, is the work of ten historians who are all distinguished authorities in their fields.

VOLUME I. ROMAN AND ANGLO-SAXON BRITAIN
   PETER SALWAY, The Open University. *Roman Britain*
   JOHN BLAIR, The Queen's College, Oxford. *The Anglo-Saxons*

VOLUME II. THE MIDDLE AGES
   JOHN GILLINGHAM, London School of Economics and Political
   Science. *The Early Middle Ages*
   RALPH A. GRIFFITHS, University College of Swansea. *The Later
   Middle Ages*

VOLUME III. THE TUDORS AND STUARTS
   JOHN GUY, University of Bristol. *The Tudor Age*
   JOHN MORRILL, Selwyn College, Cambridge. *The Stuarts*

VOLUME IV. THE EIGHTEENTH AND EARLY
    NINETEENTH CENTURIES
   PAUL LANGFORD, Lincoln College, Oxford. *The Eighteenth
   Century*
   CHRISTOPHER HARVIE, University of Tübingen. *Revolution and
   the Rule of Law*

VOLUME V. THE MODERN AGE
   H. C. G. MATTHEW, St Hugh's College, Oxford. *The Liberal Age*
   KENNETH O. MORGAN, University College of Wales, Aberystwyth.
   The Twentieth Century

THE OXFORD
MINI HISTORY
OF
BRITAIN

EDITED BY
KENNETH O. MORGAN

VOLUME II
THE MIDDLE AGES

The text of this edition first published 1984 in The Oxford Illustrated History of Britain
First issued (with revisions) as an Oxford University Press paperback 1988 in
The Oxford History of Britain
This edition produced exclusively for the Leisure Circle
by the Oxford University Press and first issued 1989
Reprinted November 1989
Reprinted April 1990

Printed and bound in Great Britain by
Cox & Wyman Ltd, Reading

CONTENTS

LIST OF MAPS

The maps on pp. 92 and 124 are based on two in *English Historical Documents*, vol. iii, by H. Rothwell, by kind permission of Methuen, London.

1. *The Early Middle Ages*

(1066–1290)

JOHN GILLINGHAM

1066 and All That

ON Christmas Day 1066 Duke William of Normandy was acclaimed king in Westminster Abbey. It was an electrifying moment. The shouts of acclamation—in English as well as in French—alarmed the Norman guards stationed outside the abbey. Believing that inside the church something had gone horribly wrong, they set fire to the neighbouring houses. Half a century later, a Norman monk recalled the chaos of that day. 'As the fire spread rapidly, the people in the church were thrown into confusion and crowds of them rushed outside, some to fight the flames, others to take the chance to go looting. Only the monks, the bishops and a few clergy remained before the altar. Though they were terrified, they managed to carry on and complete the consecration of the king who was trembling violently.'

Despite his victory at Hastings, despite the surrender of London and Winchester, William's position was still a precarious one and he had good reason to tremble. It was to take at least another five years before he could feel fairly confident that the conquest had been completed. There were risings against Norman rule in every year from 1067 to 1070: in Kent, in the south-west, in the Welsh marches, in the Fenland, and in the north. The Normans had to live like an army of occupation, living, eating, and sleeping together in operational units. They had to build castles—strong points from which a few men could dominate a subject population. There may well have been no more than 10,000 Normans living in the midst of a hostile population of one or two million. This is not to say that every single Englishman actively opposed the Normans. Unquestionably there were many who co-operated with them; it was this which made possible the successful Norman take-over of so many Anglo-Saxon institutions. But there is plenty of evidence to show that the English resented becoming an oppressed majority in their own country. The years of insecurity were to have a profound effect on subsequent history. They meant that England received not just a new royal family but also a new ruling class, a new culture and language. Probably no other conquest in European history has had such disastrous consequences for the defeated.

Almost certainly this had not been William's original intention. In the early days many Englishmen were able to offer their submission and retain their lands. Yet by 1086 something had clearly changed. Domesday Book is a record of a land deeply marked by the scars of conquest. In 1086 there were only two surviving English lords of any account. More than 4,000 thegns had lost their lands and been replaced by a group of less than 200 barons. A few of the new landlords were Bretons and men from Flanders and Lorraine but most were Normans. In the case of the Church we can put a date to William's anti-English policy. In 1070 he had some English bishops deposed and thereafter appointed no Englishman to either bishopric or abbey. In military matters, the harrying of the north during the winter of 1069–70 also suggests ruthlessness on a new scale at about this time. In Yorkshire this meant that between 1066 and 1086 land values fell by as much as two-thirds. But whenever and however it occurred it is certain that by 1086 the Anglo-Saxon aristocracy was no more and its place had been taken by a new Norman élite. Naturally this new élite retained its old lands on the Continent; the result was that England and Normandy, once two separate states, now became a single cross-Channel political community, sharing not only a ruling dynasty, but also a single Anglo-Norman aristocracy. Given the advantages of water transport, the Channel no more divided England from Normandy than the Thames divided Middlesex from Surrey. From now on, until 1204, the histories of England and Normandy were inextricably interwoven.

Since Normandy was a principality ruled by a duke who owed homage to the king of France this also meant that from now on 'English' politics became part of French politics. But the French connection went deeper still. The Normans, being Frenchmen, brought with them to England the French language and French culture. Moreover, we are not dealing with a single massive input of 'Frenchness' in the generation after 1066 followed by a gradual reassertion of 'Englishness'. The Norman Conquest of 1066 was followed by an Angevin conquest of 1153–4; although this did not involve the settlement of a Loire Valley aristocracy in England, the effect of the arrival of the court of Henry II and Eleanor of Aquitaine was to reinforce the dominance of French culture.

Whereas in 1066 less than 30 per cent of Winchester property owners had non-English names, by 1207 the proportion had risen to over 80 per cent, mostly French names like William, Robert, and Richard. This receptiveness to Continental influence means that at this time it is the foreignness of English art that is most striking. In ecclesiastical architecture, for example, the European terms 'Romanesque' and 'Gothic' describe the fashionable styles much better than 'Norman' and 'Early English'. Although churches built in England, like manuscripts illuminated in England, often contain some recognizably English elements, the designs which the architects and artists were adapting came from abroad, sometimes from the Mediterranean world (Italy, Sicily, or even Byzantium), usually from France. It was a French architect, William of Sens, who was

called in to rebuild the choir of Canterbury Cathedral after the
fire of 1174. Similarly Henry III's rebuilding of Westminster
Abbey was heavily influenced by French models. Indeed so
great was the pre-eminence of France in the fields of music,
literature, and architecture, that French became a truly international rather than just a national language, a language
spoken—and written—by anyone who wanted to consider
himself civilized. Thus, in thirteenth-century England, French
became, if anything, even more important than it had been
before. Throughout most of the period covered by this chapter
a well-educated Englishman was trilingual. English would be
his mother tongue; he would have some knowledge of Latin,
and he would speak fluent French. In this cosmopolitan society
French was vital. It was the practical language of law and estate
management as well as the language of song and verse, of
chanson and romance. The Norman Conquest, in other words,
ushered in a period during which England, like the kingdom of
Jerusalem, can fairly be described as a part of France overseas,
Outremer; in political terms, it was a French colony (though
not, of course, one that belonged to the French king) until the
early thirteenth century and a cultural colony thereafter.

It is hardly surprising, then, that generations of patriotic
Englishmen should have looked upon the battle of Hastings as
a national catastrophe. Yet even if we do not, as E. A. Freeman
did, describe Paris as 'beastly', it can still be argued that the
Norman Conquest was the greatest disaster in English history.
Not because it was predatory and destructive—though, of
course, like any conquest it was both—but because of the
problem of '1066 and All That'. With 1066 as the most famous
date in English history the Norman Conquest is a 'blessedly
well-known landmark'. It is devastatingly easy to see it as a
'new beginning' or a 'significant turning-point'. Almost everything that happened in late eleventh-century England has been
discussed in terms of the impact of the Norman Conquest. But
the second half of the eleventh century was a period of rapid

development throughout Europe. Countries which suffered no Norman Conquest were, none the less, transformed. So there is the problem. In some respects 1066 wrought great changes; in other respects, great changes occurred but can hardly be ascribed to the Conquest; in yet others, the most striking feature is not change at all, but continuity.

The main problem facing the historian of this period, however, is posed not by a single dramatic event, but by a social and cultural process of great complexity. This is the tremendous proliferation of written records which occurred during the twelfth and thirteenth centuries. Many more documents than ever before were written and many more were preserved. Whereas from the whole of the Anglo-Saxon period about 2,000 writs and charters survive, from the thirteenth century alone there are uncounted tens of thousands. Of course the 2,000 Anglo-Saxon documents were only the tip of the iceberg; many more did not survive. But this is true also of the thirteenth century. It has, for example, been estimated that as many as eight million charters could have been produced for thirteenth-century smallholders and peasants alone. Even if this were to be a rather generous estimate, it would still be true that whole classes of the population, serfs for example, were now concerned with documents in ways that previously they had not been. Whereas in the reign of Edward the Confessor only the king is known to have possessed a seal, in Edward I's reign even serfs were required by statute to have them. At the centre of this development, and to some extent its motor, lay the king's government. The king possessed permanently organized writing offices, the chancery, and then the exchequer too: they were becoming busier and busier. In Henry III's reign, we can measure the amount of sealing wax which the chancery used. In the late 1220s it was getting through 3.63 lb. per week; by the late 1260s the amount had gone up to 31.9 lb. per week. Not only was the government issuing more documents than ever before; it was also systematically making copies and keeping them. Here the key date is 1199. In that year the chancery clerks began to keep copies, on rolls of parchment, of most of the letters—and certainly of all the important ones—sent out under the great seal. The survival of the chancery enrolments means that from 1199 historians know a great deal more about the routine of government than ever before.

These are developments of fundamental importance. The proliferation of records involved a shift from habitually memorizing things to writing them down. It meant that the whole population was now, in a sense, 'participating in literacy'; even if they could not themselves read they became accustomed to seeing day-to-day business transacted through the medium of writing. Clearly this development of a literate mentality is closely linked with the cultural movement commonly known as the twelfth-century Renaissance. At first the power-houses of the new learning all lay abroad in the towns and cathedrals of Italy and France; but by the late twelfth century there were some schools of higher learning in England and by the 1220s two universities, first at Oxford and then at Cambridge, had been established. At Oxford there were schools where men could learn severely practical subjects such as conveyancing, administration, and elementary legal procedure. And throughout England the signs point to an increasing number of schools at all levels.

But are these profound developments associated with revolutionary changes in other aspects of social organization? Clearly, the production of all these written records means that society is becoming more bureaucratic, but does this mean that the relationships between classes are being conserved or being altered? Is the economic system changing? Is the political system changing? Or are both merely being more elaborately recorded?

These are not questions which it is easy to answer. The cumulative nature of the evidence tends to deceive. For example, a particular form of relationship between men may first be clearly documented in the thirteenth century. But does this mean that the relationship itself originated in that century? Or that these types of relationship were first fixed in writing then?

Or only that this is the earliest period from which the relevant documents happen to have survived? A case in point is the fact that the earliest known examples of a type of document known as the 'indenture of retainer' date from the thirteenth century. The indenture records the terms on which a man was engaged to serve his lord; it would normally specify his wages and, if it was a long-service contract, his retaining fee. On the basis of these documents, historians have decided that the 'indentured retainer' and the 'contract army' both came into existence towards the end of the thirteenth century, and that they were characteristic of the later Middle Ages, the period of 'bastard feudalism'. Yet there is clear, though indirect, evidence that both contract armies and retainers receiving fee and wages were in existence at least as early as 1100. And in general in this chapter it will be argued that there was a much higher degree of continuity in economic, political, and social organization than is often supposed. But first, before going any further, it will be useful to give a brief outline of the main events, concentrating on those events which were of greatest concern to kings.

William I (1066–1087)

After 1071, William's hold on England was fairly secure. The Welsh and the Scots gave him little trouble. Scandinavian rulers continued to look upon England with acquisitive eyes but the ever-present threat of another Viking invasion never quite materialized. From 1071 to the end of his reign most of William's attention was taken up by war and diplomacy on the Continent. Normandy was his homeland and far more vulnerable to sudden attack than was his island kingdom. Several of William's neighbours were alarmed by his new power and took every opportunity to diminish it. At their head were King Philip of France, and Count Fulk le Rechin of Anjou. Their best opportunities were provided by William's eldest son Robert (b. 1054). Recognized as the heir to Normandy as long ago as 1066, he had never been allowed to enjoy either money or power, and from 1078 onwards he became involved in a series of intrigues against his father. In quarrels between the king of France and the duke of Normandy the natural battlefield was the Vexin, a disputed territory lying on the north bank of the Seine between Rouen and Paris. The county of Maine, which William had conquered in 1063, played a similar role in the hostilities between Normandy and Anjou. Maine was to remain a bone of contention for the next two generations; the Vexin for much longer still (until 1203). Thus already in William's reign it is possible to see the political pattern which was to dominate the next century: the intermingling of family dissension and frontier dispute. In this context the circumstances of William's death are revealing. The garrison of the French fortress of Mantes made a raid into Normandy. William retaliated and while his troops sacked Mantes (July 1087) he received the injury from which he died. Robert was in rebellion at the time and chose to remain at the court of King Philip, while his younger brother William dutifully, and pointedly, was to be found in attendance at his father's bedside. On 9 September 1087, William I died. His body was carried to his great church of St. Stephen at Caen. Towards the end of his life he had grown very fat and when the attendants tried to force the body into the stone sarcophagus, it burst, filling the church with a foul smell. It was an unfortunate ending to the career of an unusually fortunate and competent king.

William II (1087–1100)

Whatever William's last wishes may have been, there was a strong presumption that the eldest son should have his father's patrimony, that is those lands which the father himself had inherited. Thus, despite his rebellion, Robert succeeded to Normandy. But a man's acquisition, the land he himself had obtained whether by purchase, marriage, or conquest, could more easily be used to provide for other members of his family. Thus England, the Conqueror's vast acquisition, was used to provide for his younger son, William. Naturally, Robert objected to this and perhaps, if it had not been for his rebellion, he would have succeeded to England as well.

What is clear is that the customs governing the succession to the throne were still flexible; they could—should—be bent in order to take account of political realities, for example the characters of the rival candidates. Thus those influential men, Archbishop Lanfranc of Canterbury among them, who decided to accept William Rufus as king of England, may well have judged that he would make a better ruler than his elder brother. In view of Robert's record both before and after 1087 this would have been a reasonable judgement, yet within a few months of his accession Rufus found himself opposed by a powerful coalition of great barons, the magnates. According to the Anglo-Norman chronicler Orderic Vitalis, the rebels' objective was to reunite England and Normandy, not for the sake of some principle of constitutional law but in order to ease their own political problems. Their dilemma was summed up in the words which Orderic placed in the mouth of the greatest of them, Odo of Bayeux. 'How can we give proper service to two distant and mutually hostile lords? If we serve Duke Robert well we shall offend his brother William and he will deprive us of our revenues and honours in England. On the other hand if we obey King William, Duke Robert will deprive us of our patrimonies in Normandy.' This was an argument which appealed to powerful vested interests and could very easily have unseated Rufus. If there were to be just one ruler of the joint Anglo-Norman realm then the elder brother's claim was difficult to deny. Fortunately for Rufus, his brother's case went almost by default: Robert stayed in Normandy, leaving his supporters in the lurch. None the less the 1088 revolt, despite its swift collapse, does reveal just how precarious was the position of a king of England who was not also duke of Normandy.

Taking the forty-eight years (1087–1135) of the reigns of William II and Henry I as a whole, it can be seen that the rebellions (1088, 1095, 1101, 1102) cluster in the two periods (some fifteen years in all) when the king was not duke, that is 1087–96 and 1100–6. Obviously, it was not in the king's interest that England and Normandy should be under separate rulers. But neither was it in the interest of the aristocracy. As Odo of Bayeux's speech makes plain they had too much at risk to welcome instability. Whenever the cross-Channel kingdom did break up into its constituent parts this ushered in a period of conflict which was only settled when one ruler ousted the other. Thus the primary concern of a king of England was to win and hold Normandy.

In 1089 Rufus laid claim to the duchy. With English silver he was able to buy support and he campaigned there with some success. But his hold on England still remained insecure; he faced a conspiracy in 1095. Next year the tension was resolved, at any rate temporarily, in a totally unforeseeable manner. The astonishing success of Pope Urban II's preaching tour created a climate of opinion in which thousands decided to join an expedition aimed at recovering Jerusalem from the Muslims. For Robert Curthose this offered an honourable and exciting way out of his increasingly difficult domestic political position. In order to equip himself and his retinue for the long march, he pawned Normandy to William for 10,000 marks.

The new duke's next task was to recover Maine and the Vexin, lost during Robert's slack rule. By 1099, this had been successfully accomplished. Rufus had restored his father's kingdom to its former frontiers; indeed in Scotland, by installing Edgar on the throne in 1097, he intervened more effectively than even his father had done.

Yet for all his success as a generous leader of soldiers, William's reputation has remained consistently low. Unfortunately for him, the history of the time was written almost entirely by monks and they did not like him. Serious-minded churchmen, accustomed to the conventional piety and sober discretion of his father's court, were appalled by Rufus's, by its ostentatious extravagance, by its gaiety, and by the new fashions—long hair for example—which seemed to them to be both effeminate and licentious. Rufus never married. According to the Welsh *Chronicle of Princes*, 'he used concubines and because of that died without an heir'. He may have been sceptical of the claims of religion—at any rate this is how contemporaries portrayed him; undoubtedly he treated the Church as a rich corporation which needed soaking. He was rarely in a hurry to appoint bishops and abbots, for during vacancies he could help himself to the Church's revenues. In carrying out these profitable policies Rufus relied on the ingenious aid of a quick-witted and worldly clerk, Ranulf Flambard, whom he eventually made bishop of Durham.

Above all Rufus's reputation has suffered because in 1093, when he thought he was dying, he appointed a saintly scholar Anselm of Bec as Archbishop of Canterbury (after having kept the see vacant for four years). What made this appointment so disastrous from William's point of view was the fact that it occurred at a time when a European movement for Church reform—the Gregorian reform—had created a controversial atmosphere in which holy men were only too likely to become political radicals. In 1095 William called a council at Rockingham to deal with the matters in dispute between him and Anselm. To the consternation of all, Archbishop Anselm appealed to Rome, arguing that as Archbishop of Canterbury he could not be judged in a secular court. The rise of the Papacy in the second half of the eleventh century, with its claim to the first loyalty of prelates, had brought a new and disturbing element on to the political stage. If churchmen were to believe that their obligations to God, as defined by the vicar of St. Peter, were to override their duty to the king, then the customary structure of the world would have been turned upside down.

Anselm's case in favour of an autonomous spiritual hierarchy was a well-reasoned one; in this respect he can be said to have had the better of the argument. But Rufus had a case too; not only that, he had power—pitted against the material resources available to a masterful king, a scholarly Archbishop of Canterbury was in a very weak position indeed. William continued to harass the archbishop, and never showed any sympathy for his attempts to reform the Church. Eventually Anselm could bear it no longer. In 1097 he sailed from Dover, leaving the estates of Canterbury to be taken into the king's hand. In the short run the king had gained from the quarrel. In 1100 he enjoyed the revenues of three bishoprics and twelve abbeys. Nor was there as yet any sign that the arguments had undermined men's belief in the awesome powers of an anointed king. Even Eadmer, the Canterbury monk who wrote a *Life of Anselm*, remarked of Rufus that 'the wind and the sea seemed to obey him'. Indeed, Eadmer went on, 'in war and in the acquisition of territory he enjoyed such success that you would think the whole world smiling upon him'. Whether, in reality, William II's position in 1100 was quite so strong is another matter; it suited moralistic chroniclers to portray him as a self-confident, boastful king who was struck down just when he seemed to be at the very pinnacle of success. During the summer of 1100 everyone must have known that the peaceful interlude of Duke Robert's absence was about to end. The crusader was on his way home, accompanied by a rich wife and basking in the prestige due to a man who had fought his way into the Holy City. When Curthose reclaimed his inheritance, who could tell what would happen or what line the Anglo-Norman magnates would take? As it happened, on 2 August 1100 a hunting accident in the New Forest brought the life of this forceful and much-maligned king to an abrupt end. Also, as it happened, William's younger brother was in the New Forest on the day the king died.

Henry I (1100–1135)

As soon as he knew Rufus was dead Henry moved fast. He rode to Winchester and took possession of the treasury. Then he went straight on to Westminster where he was crowned on 5 August. This speed of action has prompted speculation that

Henry knew that his brother was going to die, that he had 'arranged the accident'. But no contemporary makes the charge and if Henry had planned so cold-blooded a crime his timing is likely to have been different. The impending war between Rufus and Curthose could be expected to end with the defeat and perhaps the elimination of one of them. In other words a delayed assassination would have opened up to the assassin the prospect of obtaining *both* England *and* Normandy. As it was, Rufus's death in August 1100 meant that Henry had to act with phenomenal speed merely to seize control of just one of the two parts of the Anglo-Norman realm. A man capable of waiting for so long before he struck would surely have waited a year or two longer.

A few weeks later, Robert arrived back in Normandy. Henry had to prepare to meet the inevitable invasion. His policy was to buy support by granting favours and wide-ranging concessions. This was a policy proclaimed on the day of his coronation, when he issued a charter of liberties denouncing his brother's oppressive practices and promising good government. On the other hand the urgent need to organize his defences meant that Henry could not afford to cause too much confusion. This was a time for gestures and manifestos, but it was not the moment to overturn a whole regime. The reality of the situation was that his elder brother had left him a ready-made court and administration and Henry had little choice but to take them over.

When Duke Robert landed at Portsmouth in July 1101, many of the greatest barons in England, led by Robert of Bellême and his brothers, flocked to his side. But Rufus's court circle, Robert of Meulan at their head, remained loyal to Henry; so also did the English Church. Both sides drew back and negotiated. Henry was to keep England and pay his brother a pension of £2,000 a year.

Having survived the crisis of 1101, Henry set about ensuring that it would not recur. The essential first step was the overthrow of the house of Montgomery (Bellême). In 1102 he captured Robert of Bellême's chief strongholds in the Welsh marches and then banished him. Two years later he confiscated the lands of William of Mortain. But Earls Robert and William, like others in their position, possessed in their Norman properties a base from which to organize the recovery of their English lands. By perpetuating the separation of England and Normandy the treaty of 1101 had ensured the continuance of political instability. So in a rerun of the history of the previous reign we find a king of England, first on the defensive, then going over to the attack. At the battle of Tinchebray (1106) the issue was decided. Duke Robert himself was captured and spent the last twenty-eight years of his life as his brother's prisoner.

Although in the first years of his reign Henry was preoccupied with Norman affairs, he was not as free to concentrate on them as he would have liked. Traditional royal rights over the Church were threatened by the new ideas associated with the Gregorian reform movement. The reformers did not only wish to purify the moral and spiritual life of the clergy; in order to do this, they believed that it was also necessary to free the Church from secular control. The most hated symbol of this control was lay investiture, a ceremony in which a new abbot or bishop received the ring and staff of office from the hands of the secular prince who had appointed him. Although the first papal decree against lay investiture had been issued as long ago as 1059 and more prohibitions had been published since, no one in England seems to have been aware of their existence until Anselm returned in the autumn of 1100. While in exile he had learned of the papal attitude to lay investiture. Thus although he himself had been invested by Rufus in 1093 he now refused either to do homage to Henry or to consecrate those prelates whom Henry had invested. This placed the king in a difficult position. Bishops and abbots were great landowners and key figures in central and local administration; he needed their assistance and had to be sure of their loyalty. On the other hand, unlike Rufus, he was unwilling to provoke a quarrel, so for years he found it more convenient to postpone the problem rather than try to solve it. Not until 1107 was the matter settled.

Henry renounced lay investiture, but prelates were to continue to do homage for their fiefs. In practice, the king's wishes continued to be the decisive factor in the making of bishops. To some extent, it can be said that Henry gave up the form but preserved the reality of control. When Anselm died in 1109 he kept the see of Canterbury vacant for five years. Yet he had lost something and he knew it. In the fierce war of propaganda which accompanied the 'Investiture Contest' the Gregorians had insisted that the king was a layman, nothing more, and as such he was inferior to all priests, for priests were concerned with the soul and the king only with the body. The Church could no longer tolerate the old idea that anointed kings were sacred deputies of God. In giving up lay investiture Henry was acknowledging the secular nature of his office. It was an important moment in the history of kingship.

Once Normandy had been conquered and a compromise solution found to the investiture dispute, Henry's main concern was to hold on to what he had. Recognizing the threat that could come from an alienated aristocracy, he was careful to close the gap between court and magnates which Rufus had allowed to develop. In Orderic's words, 'he treated the magnates with honour and generosity, adding to their wealth and estates, and by placating them in this way, he won their loyalty.' A direct threat to Henry's position came from the claim of Curthose's young son, William Clito (b. 1102) that he, not Henry, was the rightful duke of Normandy. This rival claim, coupled with Normandy's long land frontier, meant that the duchy remained the most vulnerable part of his empire. After 1106 Henry spent more than half the rest of his reign there in opposition to the traditional enemies of the Norman dukes, notably Louis VI of France (king 1108–37), and Fulk V of Anjou (count 1109–28). He organized a protective ring of alliances—no less than eight of his illegitimate daughters were married to neighbouring princes, from Alexander of Scotland in

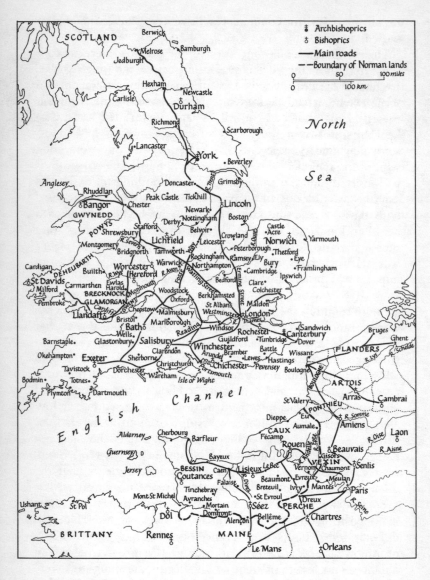

THE ANGLO-NORMAN REALM 1066–1154

Archbishoprics

Bishoprics

Main roads

Boundary of Norman lands

0   50   100 miles

0   100 km

SCOTLAND

Berwick

Melrose

Bamburgh

Jedburgh

Hexham

Carlisle

Newcastle

Durham

Richmond

Scarborough

North

Lancaster

York

Beverley

Sea

Anglesey

Rhuddlan

Doncaster

Grimsby

Bangor

Chester

Peak Castle

Tickhill

Lincoln

GWYNEDD

Newark

Boston

POWYS

Shrewsbury

Stafford

Derby

Nottingham

Belvoir

Castle Acre

Montgomery

Bridgnorth

Lichfield

Leicester

Crowland

Norwich

Yarmouth

Cardigan

DEHEUBARTH

Builth

Worcester

Warwick

Tamworth

Rockingham

Peterborough

Thetford

Eye

Framlingham

St Davids

Carmarthen

Ewias Harold

Hereford

Northampton

Ramsey

Ely

Bury

Ipswich

Milford

BRECKNOCK

Monmouth

R. Wye

Woodstock

Bedford

Cambridge

Clare

Pembroke

GLAMORGAN

Chepstow

Oxford

Berkhamsted

Colchester

Llandaff

Cardiff

Malmesbury

St Albans

Maldon

Bristol

Marlborough

Westminster

London

Bath

Reading

Windsor

Rochester

Sandwich

Wells

Salisbury

Guildford

Thames

Canterbury

Bruges

Ghent

Glastonbury

Clarendon

Winchester

Tunbridge

Dover

FLANDERS

Barnstaple

Exeter

Sherborne

Bramber

Battle

Wissant

Okehampton

Christchurch

Arundel

Chichester

Lewes

Hastings

Tavistock

Dorchester

Portsmouth

Pevensey

Boulogne

ARTOIS

Bodmin

Totnes

Wareham

Isle of Wight

Cambrai

Plympton

Dartmouth

English

Channel

St Valery

Arras

Alderney

Cherbourg

Barfleur

Dieppe

Aumale

Amiens

Laon

Guernsey

CAUX

Fécamp

Rouen

Beauvais

R. Oise

Jersey

Bayeux

Lisieux

Le Bec

VEXIN

Gisors

Senlis

BESSIN

Caen

Vernon

Chaumont

Ushant

St Pol

Coutances

Falaise

Beaumont

Evreux

Meulan

Mont St Michel

Tinchebray

Ivry

Mantes

Paris

Avranches

St Evroul

Dol

Mortain

Domfront

Séez

Dreux

PERCHE

Chartres

BRITTANY

Rennes

Alençon

Bellême

MAINE

Le Mans

Orleans

the north to Rotrou count of Perche in the south. This diplomatic pattern lends some slight credibility to William of Malmesbury's assertion that for Henry sex was a matter not of pleasure but of policy. The end result of all this activity was that Henry kept Normandy and for this reason, since it turned out to be a struggle which only maintained the status quo, historians have not been inclined to take it very seriously. But for Henry it was a very serious business indeed, a war for survival which at least once, in 1118–19, he came perilously close to losing.

The preoccupation with the defence of Normandy was a serious matter in England too, and not just for the great landowners who held estates on the Continent. Castles, garrisons, diplomacy, and war all cost a great deal of money. The connection is spelt out in the *Anglo-Saxon Chronicle*'s entry for 1118. 'King Henry spent the whole of this year in Normandy on account of the war with the king of France, count of Anjou and count of Flanders ... England paid dearly for this in numerous taxes from which there was no relief all year.' The king's long absences and his urgent need for money were the motors behind the increasing elaboration and sophistication of the machinery of government. While the king was away, England was administered by a vice-regal committee. Twice a year this committee met 'at the exchequer', that is, it met to audit the accounts of the sheriffs over the famous chequered cloth. Most of the routine administrative work, in particular the collection of revenue, was supervised by Roger of Salisbury, a man who—in contrast to the flamboyant Flambard—seems to have been the archetypal bureaucrat, competent and discreet.

The death of William, his only legitimate son, in 1120 in the wreck of the White Ship brought Henry's whole carefully contrived edifice tumbling down. From then on, the succession problem dominated the politics of the reign. Less than three months after William's death, Henry married a new wife but the heir so desperately hoped for was never born. So although Henry is said to have acknowledged more than twenty bastards, he was survived by only one legitimate child, his daughter Matilda. When her husband, Emperor Henry V of Germany, died in 1125, Henry recalled her to his court and made the barons swear to accept her as heir to the Anglo-Norman realm. Then in 1127 Henry received a fresh shock. William Clito was recognized as count of Flanders. If he were able to employ the wealth of Flanders in pursuit of his claim to Normandy, then the outlook for his uncle was black indeed. At this critical juncture Henry approached Fulk V of Anjou with a proposal for a marriage alliance between Matilda and Fulk's son and heir, Geoffrey Plantagenet. In June 1128 Matilda, somewhat against her will, was married to the fourteen-year-old youth. Unquestionably, Count Fulk had scored a diplomatic triumph: the first vital step in the Angevin take-over of the Anglo-Norman realm.

By 1135 Henry I was quarrelling openly and violently with Geoffrey and Matilda. This had the effect of driving those magnates who were loyal to Henry into opposition to the Angevins. When the old king died these magnates would inevitably find it difficult to come to terms with his designated heirs. In this sense it was Henry himself who provoked the succession dispute which followed his death. Even at the end of his life he still wanted his daughter and son-in-law to succeed, but he had been unable to bring himself to take the measures which would have enabled them to do so. Henry I had been an outstandingly able and successful king, the master politician of his age, but even he failed to cope with the tensions of the succession question. It was for this reason that Henry of Huntingdon portrayed Henry as a king in a permanent state of anxiety. 'Each of his triumphs only made him worry lest he lose what he had gained; therefore though he seemed to be the most fortunate of kings, he was in truth the most miserable.'

Stephen (1135–1154)

When the news came that Henry I lay dying, the old king's chosen heirs were in their own dominions, either in Anjou or in Maine. But his nephew, Stephen of Blois, was in his county of

Boulogne. From there, it was but a day-trip to the south-east of England. This accident of geography gave Stephen a head start. Having first secured the support of the Londoners he then rode to Winchester, where his brother, Henry of Blois, was bishop. With Henry's help he obtained both the treasury at Winchester, and Roger of Salisbury's acceptance of his claim to be king. Then all that remained was to persuade the Archbishop of Canterbury to anoint him. This was done by arguing that the oath to Matilda—which they had all sworn—was void because it had been exacted by force, and by spreading a fictitious story about the old King's deathbed change of mind. On 22 December 1135, Stephen was crowned and anointed king at Westminster.

The political structure of the Anglo-Norman realm meant that once Stephen had been recognized as king in England, he was in a very strong position in Normandy as well. From then on, the Norman barons could give their allegiance to someone else only at the risk of losing their English estates. Above all those with most to lose felt that they had to support Stephen. So, right from the start of their campaign to win their inheritance, Geoffrey and Matilda found themselves opposed by the most powerful magnates of the Anglo-Norman state.

The first two and a half years of Stephen's reign passed peacefully enough: indeed they were rather more trouble-free than the opening years of both his predecessors' reigns had been. The first serious blow came in the summer of 1138 when Robert of Gloucester decided to join his half-sister's cause. Robert's defection not only meant that Stephen lost control of some important strong points in Normandy, it was also a signal that the Angevins were on the point of carrying the struggle to England. As Stephen waited for the blow to fall he began to lose his grip on the situation.

He offended his brother Henry of Blois by not making him Archbishop of Canterbury; he arrested three influential 'civil service' bishops, including Roger of Salisbury, and thus enabled Henry of Blois to claim that ecclesiastical liberties had been infringed. In the autumn of 1139, when the Empress—as Ma-tilda was commonly known—landed at Arundel and seemed to be in Stephen's grasp, he allowed her to go free to join Robert of Gloucester at Bristol when the ruthless, if unchivalrous, thing to do was to imprison her. From now on there were two rival courts in England. The civil war was well and truly joined.

In February 1141 Stephen rashly accepted battle at Lincoln, and fought on bravely when he might have escaped. As a result, he was captured and put in prison in Bristol. Henry of Blois, now acting as papal legate, openly went over to the Empress's side and in the summer she was able to enter London. But she spurned the peace terms worked out by the legate and offended the Londoners by her tactless behaviour. When Stephen's queen, Matilda of Boulogne, advanced towards the city, the Londoners took up arms and drove the Empress out. Thus, the planned coronation at Westminster never took place. Matilda never became queen of England. A few months later Robert of Gloucester was captured and since he was the mainstay of her party Matilda had to agree to an exchange of prisoners: Stephen for Robert. The Empress had thrown away a won position; England remained a divided country.

In Normandy, events had taken a very different course. Geof-frey of Anjou stayed behind to maintain the pressure on the duchy—and to look after his own interests in Anjou. A series of campaigns from 1141 to 1144 ended with the surrender of Rouen and Geoffrey's formal investiture as duke. But the count of Anjou's single-minded concentration on the conquest of Normandy led to him turning his back on England.

Here the civil war settled down into a kind of routine. Neither side could make much headway at a time when the art of war revolved around castles, and the defenders generally held the advantage. In October 1147 Robert of Gloucester died. Disheartened, the Empress left England early in 1148, never to return.

In 1150 Geoffrey of Anjou associated his son Henry with him in the rule of the duchy. Next year this arrangement was legitimized when Louis VII (king of France 1137–80), in return for concessions in the Vexin, decided to recognize Henry as duke. At this point, it must have looked as though the old link between England and Normandy had at last been broken. Yet neither side would give up its claims and though there seemed to be a stalemate in England, on the Continent the situation turned out to be remarkably fluid. Geoffrey of Anjou died, still under forty, leaving his eldest son in control of both Normandy and Anjou. In March 1152 Louis VII divorced his wife, Eleanor of Aquitaine. Eight weeks later she married Henry Plantagenet, who in consequence could now add control of the vast duchy of Aquitaine to his other Continental possessions.

Henry's marriage was a great coup—yet it also gave fresh hope to Stephen. Louis VII organized a grand coalition of all Henry's rivals. As a result, the summer of 1152 saw Henry fighting on four fronts at once—in Aquitaine, in Normandy, against rebels in Anjou, and against Stephen in England. One well-informed Norman chronicler tells us that the betting was that Henry would not survive. At this juncture, his decision to sail to England and carry the fight to Stephen impressed contemporaries by its sheer audacity. Even so there was little Henry could do to break the stalemate in England and his whole position was still precariously over-extended when the death of Stephen's heir, Eustace, in August 1153 transformed everything. Stephen's second son, William, had never expected to be king and so the way was opened for a negotiated settlement.

The barons on both sides had long been anxious for peace. Their landed estates made them too vulnerable to the ravages of war for them to be in favour of protracted hostilities. At times they had ignored the wishes of the chief protagonists and made local truces of their own. So there was a general sense of relief when Stephen and Henry bowed to the wishes of their advisers.

By the treaty of Westminster (December 1153) it was agreed that Stephen should hold the kingdom for life and that he should adopt Henry as his heir. William was to inherit all Stephen's baronial lands. This, in essence, was a repeat of the peace terms proposed by Henry of Blois in 1141. Matilda's inability to be magnanimous in victory had cost the country another twelve years of civil war. Now at last Stephen could rule unchallenged but he was a tired man and did not live long to enjoy it. On 25 October 1154 he died and was buried by the side of his wife and elder son in the monastery they had founded at Faversham.

Stephen must take some responsibility for the troubles of his reign. He was a competent army commander and a brave knight—but perhaps too gallant for his own good. It is true that he was faced by a disputed succession, but then so were all his predecessors; disputed successions were the norm. Stephen of Blois was a more attractive character than any of the Norman kings: but he lacked their masterfulness. Without it he was unable to dominate either his court or his kingdom. Moreover he spent very little time in Normandy; only one visit, in 1137, during his entire reign. This stands in marked contrast to the itineraries of his predecessors and, in view of the 'cross-Channel structure' of the Anglo-Norman aristocracy, was certainly a mistake. In this sense the ruler from the house of Blois can be said to have failed because he was too 'English' a king to realize that England was only a part of a greater whole.

Henry II (1154–1189)

Henry took over without difficulty; it was the first undisputed succession to the English throne for over a hundred years. As lord of an empire stretching from the Scottish border to the Pyrenees he was potentially the most powerful ruler in Europe, richer even than the emperor and completely overshadowing the king of France, the nominal suzerain of his Continental possessions. Although England provided him with great wealth as well as a royal title, the heart of the empire lay elsewhere, in Anjou, the land of his fathers.

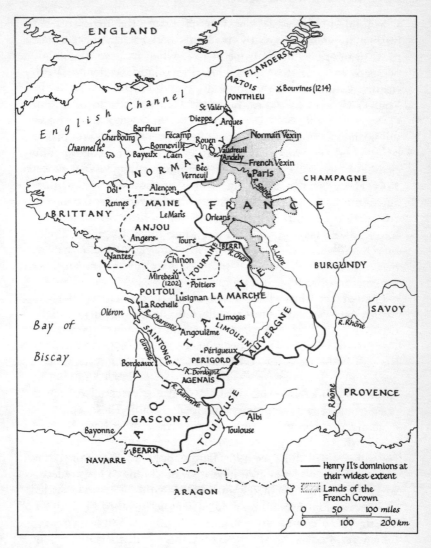

THE CONTINENTAL DOMINIONS OF HENRY II

In England his first task was to make good the losses suffered during Stephen's reign. By 1158 this had been achieved. The most dramatic example came in 1157 when he used diplomatic pressure to force the young king of Scotland, Malcolm IV, to restore Cumberland, Westmorland, and Northumbria to the English Crown. In Wales, however, Henry found in Owain of Gwynedd and Rhys of Deheubarth two well-established princes whom it was impossible to browbeat. In 1157 and 1165, force of arms proved equally unavailing in the face of a combination of Welsh guerrilla tactics and torrential summer rain. After 1165 Henry's attitude to the Welsh princes was much more accommodating. As early as 1155 he had toyed with the idea of conquering Ireland. Not until 1169–70, however, did the move into Ireland take place, first by some lords from the Welsh march and then (in 1171–2) by Henry himself. As the long delay makes plain, in the king's eyes there were matters much more urgent than the Irish question.

Out of the thirty-four years of his reign, Henry II spent twenty-one on the Continent. Socially and culturally England was a bit of a backwater compared with the French parts of the Angevin dominion. The prosperous communities which lived in the valleys of the Seine, Loire, and Garonne river systems were centres of learning, art, architecture, poetry, and music. Aquitaine and Anjou produced two of the essential commodities of medieval commerce: wine and salt. These could be exchanged for English cloth and this trade must have brought great profit to the prince who ruled over both producers and consumers. As duke of Normandy, duke of Aquitaine, and count of Anjou Henry had inherited the claims of his predecessors to lordship over neighbouring territories. These claims led to intervention in Nantes (1156) where he installed his brother, Geoffrey, as count; an expedition against Toulouse in 1159 which resulted in the capture of Cahors and the Quercy; the recovery of the Norman Vexin in 1160; and finally, as a result of repeated invasions after 1166, the occupation of Brittany and the installation of his son Geoffrey as duke.

Yet ironically it is not for his successes that Henry is best remembered, but for his dubious part in the murder of Thomas Becket. In June 1162 Becket was consecrated Archbishop of Canterbury. In the eyes of respectable churchmen Becket, who had been chancellor since 1155, did not deserve the highest ecclesiastical post in the land. He set out to prove, to an astonished world, that he was the best of all possible archbishops. Right from the start, he went out of his way to oppose the king who, chiefly out of friendship, had promoted him. Inevitably it was not long before Henry began to react like a man betrayed. In the mid-twelfth century Church-State relations bristled with problems which could be, and normally were, shelved by men of goodwill but which could provide a field-day for men who were determined to quarrel. Henry chose the question of 'criminous clerks' as the issue on which to settle accounts with his archbishop. Like many laymen, Henry resented the way in which clerks who committed felonies could escape capital punishment by claiming trial in an ecclesiastical court. At a council held at Westminster in October 1163 Henry demanded that criminous clerks should be unfrocked by the Church and handed over to the lay courts for punishment. In opposing this, Becket carried his episcopal colleagues with him but when Pope Alexander III asked him to adopt a more conciliatory line, Henry summoned a council to Clarendon (January 1164). He presented the bishops with a clear statement of the king's customary rights over the Church—the Constitutions of Clarendon—and required from them a promise to observe these customs in good faith. Taken by surprise, Becket argued for two days and then gave in. But no sooner had the rest of the bishops followed his example than Becket repented of his weakness. Thoroughly exasperated, Henry now decided to destroy Becket. He summoned him before the royal court to answer trumped-up charges. The archbishop was found guilty and sentenced to the forfeiture of his estates. In a hopeless position Becket fled across the Channel and appealed to the pope. By taking a stand on principle and then wavering Becket had reduced the English Church to confusion.

With Becket in exile Henry concentrated on more important matters for the next five years: Brittany was conquered and the English judicial system overhauled. Then in 1169 the question of the coronation of the heir to the throne, Prince Henry, led to the interminable negotiations between king, pope, and archbishop being treated as a matter of urgency. In 1170 Becket returned to England determined to punish those who had taken part in the young king's coronation. His enemies lost no time in telling Henry of the archbishop's ostentatious behaviour. 'Will no one rid me of this turbulent priest?' Henry's heated words were taken all too literally by four of his knights. Anxious to win the king's favour they rushed off to Canterbury; and there, on 29 December 1170, Becket was murdered in his own cathedral. The deed shocked Christendom and secured Becket's canonization in record time. In popular memory the archbishop came to symbolize resistance to the oppressive authority of the State, but in reality everyone was better off with him out of the way. Once the storm of protest had died down it became apparent that the king's hold on his vast empire had in no way been shaken by the Becket controversy. In the early 1170s Henry stood at the height of his power.

By this date Henry II had already decided that after his death his dominions should be partitioned between his three eldest sons. Henry was to have his father's inheritance, namely Anjou, Normandy, and England; Richard was to have his mother's inheritance, Aquitaine; Geoffrey was to have the acquisition, Brittany. For the moment there was nothing for John but later, in 1185, he was granted his father's other major acquistion, Ireland. By then Henry II's partition plans had already run into difficulties. The trouble was that they aroused expectations which, while he retained all real power in his own hands, he could not satisfy. Thus from 1173 onwards Henry was plagued by rebellious sons. The rebels, moreover, could always count on a warm welcome at the court of the king of France. After 1180 this was a serious matter for in that year the mild-mannered Louis VII was succeeded by his son Philip II Augustus, an unscrupulous politician determined to destroy the

Angevin Empire. The deaths of two of his sons, the young King Henry in 1183 and Geoffrey in 1186, ought to have simplified Henry's problems, but this was offset by the old King's obvious preference for John, a preference which alarmed Richard. An alliance between Richard and Philip brought Henry to his knees and, defeated, the old king died at Chinon on 6 July 1189.

Only in the last weeks of his life had the task of ruling his immense territories been too much for Henry. He rode ceaselessly from one corner of his empire to another, almost giving an impression of being everywhere at once—an impression that helped to keep men loyal. Although the central government offices, chamber, chancery, and military household, travelled around with him, the sheer size of the empire inevitably stimulated the further development of localized administrations which could deal with routine matters of justice and finance in his absence. Thus in England, as elsewhere, government became increasingly complex and bureaucratic. This development, taken together with Henry's interest in rational reform, has led to him being regarded as the founder of the English common law, and as a great and creative king, but in his own eyes these were matters of secondary importance. To him what really mattered was family politics and he died believing that he had failed. But for over thirty years he had succeeded.

Richard I (1189–1199)

Richard's alliance with Philip Augustus meant that his position as heir to all his father's rights and dominions was unchallengeable. John remained lord of Ireland; in time, Brittany would belong to Geoffrey's posthumous son Arthur, now two years old. The rest was at Richard's disposal.

But Richard had no wish to stay long in England. He had been made duke of Aquitaine in 1172 and since then had spent most of his life on the Continent. Even after he became king of England he was well aware that he ruled much more than England. In consequence he, like his father, had wider interests

and greater responsibilities. One aspect of this was the assistance he gave to the kingdom of Jerusalem, a kingdom ruled by
a daughter of the junior branch of the house of Anjou now
married to one of his Aquitanian vassals. In November 1187, as
soon as he heard the news of Saladin's overwhelming victory at
Hattin, Richard took the cross. Delayed by his involvement in
the family quarrels at the end of his father's reign, he was now
determined to leave for the East as soon as he had raised
enough money and arranged for the secure government of all
his dominions during a prolonged absence.

In July 1190 he and Philip Augustus set out on the Third
Crusade. Not until March 1194 did Richard again set foot on
English soil. In the mean time he had taken both a fleet and an
army to the other end of the Mediterranean. Although unable
to recapture Jerusalem, he achieved an astonishing amount
against a great opponent, Saladin. On crusade Richard tackled
and solved far greater logistical problems than ever confronted
other warrior-kings of England, William I, Edward III, or
Henry V. The treaty of Jaffa which he negotiated in 1192 enabled
the crusader states to survive for another century.

During his absence on crusade there had been some disturbances in England in 1191 but his contingency plans restored
stable government. King Philip, after his own return to France,
tried to take advantage of Richard's continued absence, but
without success. If Richard had returned from crusade as he
expected in January 1193 he would have found his empire
intact.

The damage was done while he was held captive in Germany.
He stayed in prison for more than a year (December 1192–
February ·1194) and—for all anyone knew in 1193—might have
had to stay there much longer. Even in these inauspicious
circumstances Richard's agents in England were able to contain
his younger brother's treacherous revolt. The real losses were
suffered on the Continent, in particular in Normandy where
Philip overran the Vexin and came close to capturing Rouen
itself.

Richard was released in February 1194 after payment of

100,000 marks, the first two-thirds of the king's ransom. After a brief visit to England (March–May 1194) he returned to the Continent and devoted the next five years to the hard grind of recovering the territory lost so rapidly while he was in prison. By the end of 1198 Richard's skilful diplomacy, fine generalship, and, above all, his greater resources meant that he had succeeded in recapturing almost everything that had been lost. Then, in April 1199, Richard died as the result of a wound suffered at the siege of Chalus-Chabrol (near Limoges) where he was engaged in suppressing a rebellion led by the count of Angoulême and the viscount of Limoges. In the Angevin-Capetian struggle this was to be the decisive turning-point.

One of the marks of Richard's greatness had been his ability to choose ministers, above all, Hubert Walter in England. As justiciar, Archbishop of Canterbury, and papal legate Hubert Walter stood for harmonious co-operation between king and Church. In England, as in the other provinces of the Angevin Empire, Richard's long absences meant the continuing development, under Walter's supervision, of an effective machinery of central government. From the point of view of Richard's subjects, this meant increasingly heavy taxation, but there is no evidence to suggest that the financial burdens of war had brought the Angevin Empire to the point of economic collapse.

John (1199–1216)

Richard left no legitimate children, and when he died the different parts of the Angevin Empire chose different successors. The barons of England and Normandy opted for John; Anjou, Maine, and Touraine preferred Arthur of Brittany, now twelve years old; Aquitaine continued to be held—on John's behalf— by his mother, Eleanor (d. 1204). By May 1200 John had ousted Arthur and had established himself as lord of all the Angevin dominions, though at a heavy price—the cession of the Vexin and Evreux to King Philip (treaty of Le Goulet, January 1200). Later that year his first marriage was annulled and he married

Isabella of Angoulême. There were great strategic advantages to be gained from marrying the heiress to Angoulême and had John given her fiancé, Hugh of Lusignan, adequate compensation, all might yet have been well. As it was, this marriage set in motion a train of events which led to Hugh appealing to the court of France and, in 1202, to Philip's declaration that all John's Continental dominions—the lands which he held as fiefs of the king of France—were forfeit. The sentence still had to be enforced. In 1152 Henry II had resisted Louis VII's attempt to execute a similar verdict. In 1203–4, however, John failed where his father had succeeded. By his tactless treatment of the leading barons of Anjou and Poitou he threw away all the advantages he won when he captured Arthur at Mirebeau (July 1202); the well-founded rumour that he was responsible for his nephew's murder (April 1203) further undermined an already shaky reputation. In an atmosphere of suspicion and fear John found it impossible to organize an effective defence. In December 1203 he threw in the towel and withdrew to England. Philip overran Normandy, Anjou, Maine, Touraine, and all of Poitou except for La Rochelle. These humiliating military reverses earned for John a new nickname. 'Lackland' now became 'Softsword'.

Until December 1203 John, like his father and brother, spent most of his reign in his Continental possessions. After that date he became, by force of circumstances, an English king. Not since Stephen's reign had the country seen so much of its ruler, but there was little pleasure or profit to be got from a king who constantly suspected that men were plotting against him. The weight of John's presence was even felt in the north where men were not accustomed to visits from kings of England. The extent of their resentment can be measured by the number of northerners who opposed John in 1215–16. Undoubtedly he faced genuine problems. He was duty-bound to try to recover his lost inheritance, but the conquests of 1203–4 meant that the French king was now a much more formidable opponent. An unusually high rate of inflation meant that many families and religious houses were in financial difficulties and they found it easier to blame the king than to understand the underlying economic forces. Inflation tended to erode the real value of royal revenues. As a result, John levied frequent taxes and tightened up the laws governing the forest (a profitable but highly unpopular source of income).

John also quarrelled with the Church. A disputed election to the see of Canterbury in 1205 led to a clash with Innocent III. In 1208 Innocent laid an interdict on England and Wales; all church services were suspended and remained so for six years. In 1209 John himself was excommunicated. Neither John nor lay society in general seem to have been very worried by this state of affairs; indeed since John's response to the interdict was to confiscate the estates of the Church it even helped to ease his financial problem. But in 1212 a baronial plot and Philip's plans to cross the Channel served to remind John that an excommunicated king was particularly vulnerable to rebellion and invasion. So he decided to make peace with the Church in order to have a free hand to deal with his more dangerous enemies. By agreeing to hold England as a fief of the Papacy in May 1213 he completely won over Innocent and assured himself of the pope's support in the coming struggles.

All now turned on the outcome of John's attempt to recover his lost lands. In 1214 he led an expedition to Poitou but the defeat of his allies at the battle of Bouvines (July 1214) entailed both the failure of his Continental strategy and the onset of rebellion in England. But rebels had genuine problems too. Leadership was normally provided by a discontented member of the royal family. After the elimination of Arthur, John faced no such rivals. His own sons were too young. The only possible candidate was Louis, son of Philip Augustus, but a Capetian prince was hardly an attractive anti-king. So the rebels devised a new kind of focus for revolt: a programme of reform. In June 1215, after they had captured London, the rebels forced John to accept the terms laid out in a document later to be known as Magna Carta. In essence it was a hostile commentary on some of the more objectionable features of the last sixty years of Angevin rule. As such it was clearly unacceptable to John who regarded the agreement made at Runnymede merely as a means of buying time. Attempts to implement Magna Carta only led to further quarrels. In the end the rebels had to invite Louis to take the throne. In May 1216 he entered London. When John died, in October 1216, shortly after losing part of his baggage train in quicksands in the Wash, the country was torn in two by a civil war which was going badly for the Angevins.

John possessed qualities which have endeared him to some modern historians. He took a close interest in the details of governmental and legal business, but in his own day this counted for little. It is a mistake to see him as a busier king than his predecessors. The survival of chancery records from 1199 onwards permits historians to look, for the first time, into the daily routine of the king's government at work. As a result they have sometimes given the impression that John was unusually competent. In fact he was a very poor king, incompetent where it really mattered, in the management of his more powerful subjects.

Henry III (1216–1272)

The minority council which governed in the name of John's nine-year-old son, Henry, was soon vouchsafed that success in war, both on land (the battle of Lincoln, May 1217) and at sea (battle of Dover, August 1217), which had been denied his father. Under the impact of these defeats, support for Louis dwindled rapidly. In September 1217 he accepted the treaty of Lambeth and withdrew.

It was not until 1232 that Henry began to rule in his own right. Minorities tended to be periods of unstable government; but, on the whole, the men, above all Hubert de Burgh, who kept Henry in political tutelage until he was in his mid-twenties, did remarkably well. Most of the struggles for power took place in the council chamber; appeals to arms were rare and very brief. As part of a series of conciliatory moves Magna Carta was amended and reissued. But while the lords of the council concentrated on their own rivalries and on events in England and Wales, they were understandably less concerned about the king's overseas inheritance. None of them had estates in Poitou and Gascony. In 1224, during one such domestic quarrel, their old Capetian enemy, now King Louis VIII, walked into Poitou, captured La Rochelle, and threatened Gascony. An expedition in 1225 consolidated the position in Gascony but made no serious attempt to recover Poitou. Subsequent expeditions, in 1230 and 1242, were on a more ambitious scale but ended ingloriously. After 1224, only Gascony remained of the lands which Henry III's ancestors had once held in France. The effect of this was to reverse the territorial balance of the twelfth century. Once England had been one of the provinces in the Angevin orbit; now it became the indisputable centre of the Plantagenet dominions. Eventually, by the treaty of Paris (1259), Henry gave up his claims to Normandy, Anjou, and Poitou, and did homage to Louis IX for Gascony.

Realistically speaking, the treaty of Paris was Henry III's greatest political success but he accepted the generous terms offered by Louis IX only with great reluctance and in the hope of extricating himself from his other difficulties. Chief among these was the fact that a sworn confederation of the most powerful magnates in the country was threatening to take up arms against him. Henry had faced opposition on and off since 1233. Time and again, the bone of contention had been his choice of friends and advisers; these were the men who obtained the lion's share of the patronage at the king's disposal. The problem was aggravated by the fact that many of his favourites were not English—this at a time when English politics were becoming increasingly insular. Henry was a good family man, happily married (since 1236) to Eleanor of Provence, and ready to provide generously for his wife's relatives. Then, when life in France became difficult for his half-brothers, the Lusignans—his mother's children by her second marriage—

he welcomed them to England and from 1247 onwards they constantly soured the atmosphere.

Equally controversial was the king's scheme for providing for Edmund, his own second son. In 1252 the pope offered the kingdom of Sicily to Henry and in 1254 he accepted on Edmund's behalf. Unfortunately, Sicily was actually held by Manfred, an illegitimate son of the Hohenstaufen Emperor Frederick II. Not only did Henry agree that he would finance the island's conquest, he also promised to meet the pope's existing debts—and the pope had already spent a fortune, some 135,000 marks, in fighting Manfred. It was an absurd commitment and in 1258 it ended with the barons taking the government out of the king's hands and initiating a far-reaching programme of reform: the Provisions of Oxford (October 1258) and the Provisions of Westminster (October 1259). But taking power out of the hands of an adult king, and handing it to an elected aristocratic council, was a revolutionary step. For the next five years England teetered on the brink of civil war. When, in the spring of 1264, war finally came, the issues at stake had been narrowed down to one question. Was, or was not, the king free to choose foreigners to be his counsellors? Ironically, the man who had been most adamant in insisting that in the last resort it was the barons, acting in the name of 'the community of the realm', who should decide, was himself born a foreigner, Simon de Montfort. By this time, Simon had long been a powerful member of 'the community': earl of Leicester since 1231, husband of the king's sister since 1238. In 1264 Earl Simon won the battle of Lewes, but next year was himself defeated, killed, and dismembered at the battle of Evesham. In the last years of Henry III's reign the full restoration of royal authority was combined with the recognition, in the statute of Marlborough (1267), that the 'customs of the realm' including both Charters of Liberties and even some of the Provisions of Westminster, should be upheld. Feeling uncomfortable in this atmosphere of moderation, the victor of Evesham, Edward, the heir to the throne, went off on crusade, leaving his father free to concentrate on rebuilding Westminster Abbey.

Edward I (1272–1307)

In 1272 Edward I was in Sicily, on his way back from crusade, when he heard the news that his father had died and that he had been proclaimed king. He returned home at a leisurely pace. In Paris, choosing his words carefully, he did homage to Philip III for his lands in France: 'I do you homage for all the lands which I ought to hold of you.' He then turned south to Gascony where he stayed in 1273–4. He visited Gascony again in 1286–9. He was the last Plantagenet king to hold court at Bordeaux and when he left, in July 1289, it marked the end of an era. Yet the history of English rule in Gascony is by no means a straightforward story of decline. In 1279, for example, the French at last handed over the Agenais, as they were bound to do under the terms of the treaty of Paris. The Agenais was an important wine-growing area and its cession further strengthened the rapidly-developing commercial links between Bordeaux and London. The Bordeaux wine customs, farmed for only £300 a year in the 1240s, were worth over £6,000 sixty years later. In return the Gascons imported English cloth, leather, and corn. A mutual interest in an expanding trade riveted the two communities together.

In October 1274, soon after his return to England, Edward launched an inquiry into the activities of both royal and baronial officials. Like similar earlier investigations it uncovered an enormous number of grievances and in trying to remedy some of these, the king's advisers, headed by his chancellor, Robert Burnell, were led on to issue new laws on a wide range of subjects. But even in the most prolific period of legislation (1275–90) there was no attempt to codify English law in the manner of a Justinian and the statutes were quite as much concerned with the rights of the king as with the liberties of the subject.

From 1276 to 1284 Edward's main preoccupation was with

Wales. Initially his plan was to cut Llywelyn ap Gruffydd down to size and then hand the Welsh prince's lands to his brothers Dafydd and Gruffydd. But after the victorious campaign of 1277 he imposed a peace treaty which the Welsh found humiliating and failed to give Dafydd the rewards he had expected. In 1282 the Welsh rebelled. In the war of 1282–3 Llywelyn was killed and Dafydd captured. He was then put on trial and executed as a traitor, the first man since 1076 to forfeit his life for rebellion. Unlike the campaign of 1277, the war of 1282–3 had been intended as a war of conquest; given Edward's enormous preponderance of resources, it was not too difficult a task.

Whereas the conquest of Wales can be seen as the culmination of centuries of warfare, relations between the kingdoms of England and Scotland were exceptionally good for most of the thirteenth century. But in 1286 Alexander III was killed by a fall from his horse and his only granddaughter, Margaret, the 'Maid of Norway', was recognized as heir to the throne. Edward I proposed that she should marry his own son and heir, Edward. The Scottish magnates agreed to this proposal (treaty of Birgham, July 1290) but at the same time insisted that Scotland should retain its own laws and customs.

Sadly, the six-year-old Margaret died in Orkney (September 1290). Edward seized the opportunity to assert his overlordship and his right to adjudicate between the contenders for the throne. After complicated legal arguments he decided in favour of John Balliol; on St. Andrew's Day 1292 the new king was enthroned at Scone. Up to this point Edward was justified in claiming that his actions had helped to maintain peace and order in Scotland; but from now on his domineering treatment of the Scots was to provoke a long and disastrous war.

Wales and the Marches

Eleventh-century Wales was a collection of small kingdoms in a mountainous country. These were kingdoms without stable borders. They expanded and contracted in accordance with law (the custom of sharing the inheritance between sons) and politics (the ambitions and military fortunes of individual rulers). Although English kings traditionally claimed an overall supremacy here, they had done little to transform that ill-defined overlordship into lasting military and administrative control. At first it looked as though the impetus of the Norman Conquest of England would carry the newcomers right through Wales. The Norman earls of Hereford, Shrewsbury, and Chester were, in effect, licensed to take whatever they could. But after a period of rapid advance in 1067–75, they found their progress impeded by the nature of the terrain. As a result, their colonizing efforts were long confined to the lowlands and river valleys, particularly in the south. There were indeed periods when Welsh princes recovered the initiative and resumed control of lands they had earlier lost. Not until the reign of Edward I was the Norman Conquest of Wales complete. Thus throughout this period Wales was a land of war, a land of castles. Welsh princes and Anglo-Norman marcher lords made war and peace and both therefore enjoyed what later constitutional lawyers would call 'sovereign' powers.

For most of this period the conquest was a piecemeal affair, undertaken and carried through by individual Anglo-Norman baronial families: the Clares, the Mortimers, the Lacys, the Braoses. The lands which they conquered were, in effect, 'private' lordships, outside the normal framework of English governance. Nonetheless, these families remained subjects of the king of England and occasionally they were reminded of this fact in summary fashion. In 1102 Henry I broke the sons of Roger of Montgomery, earl of Shrewsbury, and dismembered their father's marcher 'empire'. In 1208–11 John drove William de Braose to destruction. The groundwork of conquest and colonization was left to the marcher lords, but the overall strategy remained in royal hands. It was, for example, the kings who determined what relations with the native princes should be: a matter which became increasingly vital as some Welsh kingdoms were eliminated and the surviving ones became increasingly consolidated.

By the second half of the twelfth century the rulers of Deheubarth, particularly the Lord Rhys, and of Gwynedd were outstanding. In the thirteenth century two princes of Gwynedd, Llywelyn the Great and his grandson, Llywelyn ap Gruffydd, managed, by force and diplomacy, to bring all the other Welsh dynasties under their authority. Indeed in the treaty of Montgomery (1267) Llywelyn ap Gruffydd was able to persuade a reluctant English king, Henry III, to acknowledge both his territorial gains and his new title, 'Prince of Wales'.

But eight years earlier another treaty had sealed the fate of Wales. In 1259 by the treaty of Paris Henry III accepted the loss of most of his Continental possessions. Peace with France meant that for the first time a king of England could, if he wanted to, concentrate his attention on his British neighbours. There followed Edward's conquest and a massive programme of castle building. By the statute of Wales (1284) the newly-acquired lands were divided into shires on the English model: Flint, Anglesey, Merioneth, and Caernarfon. As for Welsh laws and customs, Edward announced: 'certain of them we have abolished; some we have allowed, some we have corrected, others we have added'. What this meant in effect was that English common law had been introduced into Wales.

There were revolts in 1287 and 1294–5 but the castles proved their worth. Flint, Rhuddlan, Aberystwyth, Builth, Conway, Caernarfon, Criccieth, Harlech, and Beaumaris—resounding names, and resoundingly expensive to build and maintain. This was the high premium Edward paid to insure his conquests against the fire of rebellion.

The contrast between, on the one hand, the piecemeal conquest of the south and east and, on the other, the sudden defeat which overwhelmed the north and west left an enduring mark on the political geography of Wales. The Edwardian conquests were largely retained in Crown hands; the rest remained divided into the numerous large lordships collectively known as the march of Wales. As for Prince Llywelyn, killed in an English trap at Irfon Bridge in 1282, his fate was to become a cult figure for some twentieth-century Welsh nationalists.

Scotland

In contrast to fragmented Wales, in the eleventh century much of Scotland, in particular the south and east—the wealthiest part—was ruled by one king, the king of the Scots. Ever since Athelstan's reign, the king of the Scots had occasionally recognized English overlordship, but that was as far as the connection went—or was likely to go. On the one hand the king of the Scots was too powerful to have much to fear from the kind of 'private enterprise' invasions which marked the advance of Anglo-Norman barons into Wales and even Ireland. On the other, his land was too poor and he was generally too distant a figure to be of much interest to the kings of England. Besides, although it might not be too difficult to launch a successful expedition against the Scots, the dual problem of conquering and controlling so remote a country seemed—and probably was—insoluble to kings whose own bases lay in the Thames Valley and further south.

Nor were the Scots obsessed by the problem of the English. Apart from a temporary success when King David (1124–53) took advantage of the civil war of Stephen's reign to acquire Northumbria (held from 1149 to 1157), the border with England effectively remained where it had been established in the eleventh century. Much more significant was the kingdom's extension to include the far north and much of the western seaboard (Caithness, Ross, Moray, Argyll, Galloway). The culmination of this expansionist policy came when the king of Norway ceded the Western Isles (treaty of Perth, 1266). Scottish advance here was materially assisted by the stability and continuity of leadership provided by three successive kings: William I (1165–1214), Alexander II (1214–49), and Alexander III (1249–86).

Territorial expansion in the Highlands was matched by internal development in the Lowlands. Here, burghs, abbeys, and cathedrals were founded; castles were built and royal sheriffdoms formed in order to reduce the kingdom to manageable administrative units; royal moneyers began to mint silver pennies (enjoying parity with English sterling) and import duties were collected. The marriages made by its rulers show that in the twelfth and thirteenth centuries Scotland was increasingly becoming part of a 'European' political scene. What was most remarkable about all these developments was that they involved very little war. So long as no English king conceived the un-realistic ambition of conquering Scotland, there was no reason for that to change.

Government

The most important component of government remained the king himself. His character still counted for more than any other single factor—as is obvious from the contrast between Edward I's reign and the reigns of both his father and son. But naturally the king could not govern alone. Wherever he went he was followed by a great crowd: courtiers, officials, servants, traders, petitioners, and hangers-on of every description.

At the centre of the crowd that followed him was the king's household. In part this was an elaborate domestic service: cooks, butlers, larderers, grooms, tent-keepers, carters, pack-horse drivers, and the bearer of the king's bed. There were also the men who looked after his hunt, the keepers of the hounds, the horn-blowers, the archers. Then there were the men whose work was political and administrative as well as domestic. Some of them had fairly well-defined functions. The chancellor was responsible for the king's seal and the chancery clerks. Treasurer and chamberlains looked after the king's money and valuables. Constables and marshals were in charge of military organization. But the household, like the king, was omni-competent and any great household officer, the steward for example, was likely to find himself entrusted with essential political and military tasks.

Some of these officials were clerks. Until the 1340s the chan-cellor and the treasurer always were. But many of them were laymen: the chamberlains, the stewards, the constables, the marshals—as also, at a local level, were the sheriffs. Medieval kings of England did not depend exclusively, or even primarily, upon clerks for the administrative skills necessary to rule a country. Nor did they rely on a group of royal officials whose interests were pitted against the interests of the great land-holders, the magnates. On the contrary, the king's household normally included some of the most powerful barons. Servants in the king's household, they were also lords of great estates and masters in their own houses. Through their influence the authority of the Crown was carried into the localities. This in-formal power system was often reinforced by the appointment of members of the household to local offices. Under Rufus, Hamo 'the steward' was sheriff of Kent; Urse d'Abetôt was constable of the household and sheriff of Worcester. Throughout the twelfth and thirteenth centuries household knights continued to be employed as sheriffs.

Here, in the king's household, lay the mainspring of govern-ment. This is as true of 1279, the year of Edward I's Household Ordinance, as it is of 1136, the approximate date of the earliest surviving description of the king's household, the *Constitutio domus regis*. Moreover there is no reason to believe that the household of the *Constitutio* was significantly different from William I's household, or indeed, from Cnut's household.

Similarly the king's household was the hub of military organ-ization. It has long been accepted that the armies of Edward I's reign were essentially 'the household in arms'. The house-hold cavalry constituted a professional task force capable of responding quickly if trouble blew up unexpectedly. In the event of a major campaign, it could be rapidly expanded. Household knights were often made responsible for mobilizing and commanding large infantry contingents. The household men, the *familiares*, were paid annual fees and then daily wages according to the number of days they served. This, it used to be thought, was a far cry from the Norman period when armies were basically 'feudal hosts', made up of the quotas of knights which tenants-in-chief mustered when summoned to perform their military service to the Crown. But close study of the much more fragmentary evidence for the period around 1100 has demonstrated that not only is it difficult to find the 'feudal host' in action, but also that all the essential features of the Edwardian system were already in existence—the retaining fees, the daily wages, the framework for planned expansion, the use of household troops both as garrisons for key castles and as the main field armies (composed of knights and mounted archers), the employment of household knights as commanders of supplementary forces. There is no reason to believe that the tasks which Cnut's housecarls were called upon to perform were fundamentally different.

For practical purposes there was an upper limit on the size of the royal household in peacetime; transport and catering problems were alone sufficient to see to that. To some extent, forward planning of the royal itinerary helped; when they knew in advance where the household was going to be then merchants could arrange to be there with their wares. But the presence of the king imposed a near-intolerable burden on any district through which he passed. The demands made by the household had a dramatic effect on local foodstocks and prices; it created a situation wide open to abuse. This is how Eadmer, a monk of Canterbury, described the household of William Rufus, a king of whom he disapproved. 'Those who attended his court made a practice of plundering and destroying everything; they laid waste all the territory through which they passed. Consequently when it became known that the king was coming everyone fled to the woods.' In Edward I's reign there is still the same combination of planning and plunder. An official letter announcing that he intended to spend Easter at Nottingham asked that local people should be comforted by being assured that the king would go as fast as he had come.

Thus it was both for political reasons—in order to make his presence felt—and for economic reasons—to make his presence no longer felt—that the king travelled constantly. The sheer size of their dominions meant that in this respect the Angevins had to work harder than their predecessors, though John's political failures did at least have the effect of easing his travel problems. After 1203 the royal itinerary became increasingly confined to England and, in Edward I's case, to North Wales as well. After 1289 no king visited Gascony. At the same time the roads leading in and out of London became gradually more import- ant. By 1300 the king's itinerary was no longer dominated, as John's had still been, by the restless move from palace to hunting lodge in 'central Wessex', the old heartland of the West Saxon kings.

Yet while political and economic considerations made the court mobile, there was another feature of the age which pointed in the opposite direction: the seemingly inexorable development of bureaucracy. Given the practical limitations on household size, what would happen as the king's secretarial and financial officers grew ever more numerous? Inevitably not all of them could continue to travel everywhere with their lord. Some were bound to settle down in a convenient place. By 1066 indeed this point had already been reached. There was already a permanent royal treasury at Winchester, a depository for fiscal records as well as for silver, and this required a perman- ent staff to guard and oversee it. By 1290 there were many more settled officials, both clerks and laymen, in the chancery and exchequer, and they were settled at Westminster, not Win- chester. But this bureaucratic growth had not altered the fun- damental political facts of life: the king still itinerated; he still took with him a seal, a secretariat, and financial experts—and it was within this mobile group, not at Westminster, that the most important political and administrative decisions were taken. In 1290, as in 1066, the saddle remained the chief seat of government, both in war and in peace. There was still no capital but the king's highway.

Nor had bureaucratic growth altered the basic fact that the political stability of the realm still depended primarily on the king's ability to manage the small, but immensely powerful, aristocratic establishment—as is made clear by the events of Henry III's and Edward II's reign. On what terms did the tenants-in-chief hold their estates from the king? They were expected—as they had been in Anglo-Saxon England—to serve and aid the king: essentially this meant political service and, in times of war, military service; in certain circumstances they could be asked to give him financial aid. In addition, a tenant-in-chief's heir had to pay a duty, known as a relief, in order to enter into his inheritance, while if he—or she—were under age then the king took the estates into his custody, to do with them very much as he pleased (subject to certain conventions). In these circumstances the king controlled his ward's marriage. If there were no direct heirs, then after provision had been made for the widow—whose re-marriage was also subject to Crown control—the king could grant the land out again to whomever be pleased. This degree of control over the inheritances and marriages of the wealthiest people in the kingdom meant that the king's powers of patronage were immense. He not only had offices at his disposal, he also had heirs, heiresses, and widows. Thus, for example, when Richard I gave William Marshal the heiress to the earldom of Pembroke, he, in effect, made William a millionaire overnight. No political leader in the Western world of today has anything remotely approaching the power of patronage in the hands of a medieval king. It is not surprising that the king's court was the focal point of the whole political system, a turbulent, lively, tense, factious place in which men—and a few women—pushed and jostled each other in desperate attempts to catch the king's eye. Not surprisingly it was a twelfth-century literary convention to describe a courtier's life as sheer hell—but standing at the mouth of hell there were hundreds only too keen to enter. In these circumstances patronage was one of the strongest cards in the king's hand. It mattered how he played it, and a king who played it badly would soon find himself in trouble.

The essential features of this patronage system were already in existence during the reign of William Rufus. This much is clear from the terms of the Coronation Charter issued by Henry I in 1100. It is also clear that the system was still in existence during the reign of Edward I. Magna Carta had clarified it and, to some extent, even modified it. After 1215, for example, baronial reliefs were fixed at a rate of £100. None the less, the laws governing inheritance, wardship, and marriage could still be manipulated to suit a king's personal predilections, whether it was to provide for his own family, as with Edward I, or to enrich favourites, as with Edward II. What is less clear is whether the system was already there in 1066. Most historians would probably say that it was not. But it is surely significant that Cnut and, probably, Æthelred the Unready were already making promises broadly similar to those contained in the charter of 1100.

Patronage was lucrative. Men offered money in order to obtain what the king had to offer: offices (from the chancellorship down), succession to estates, custody of land, wardship, and marriage—or even nothing more concrete than the king's goodwill. All of these were to be had at a price, and the price was negotiable. Here was an area in which a king could hope to raise more money by consistently driving harder bargains. In these circumstances any document which told the king how rich his tenants were would naturally be immensely valuable. Domesday Book is just such a record—and it showed that half the value of the whole country was in the hands of less than two hundred men. By fining these men heavily when they were in political trouble or by offering them what they wanted, though at a price, the king had found a practical method of soaking the rich. Of course the information had to be kept up to date and throughout the twelfth and thirteenth centuries the Crown found ways of ensuring that it was. For example, one of the surviving documents produced by Henry II's administration is the delightfully named 'Roll of Ladies, boys and girls'. Thus to a hostile observer like Gerald of Wales the king appeared to be 'a robber permanently on the prowl, always probing, always looking for the weak spot where there is something for him to steal'. Gerald was talking of the position under the Angevins but it may be that Lucy, widowed countess of Chester, offering

Henry I 500 marks for the privilege of remaining single for five years, would have concurred. The fact that most of the influential people in the realm were semi-permanently in their debt gave kings a powerful political lever—and one which they regularly employed. In 1295, for example, Edward I used the threat of debt collection to force a group of reluctant magnates to go to Gascony.

The earliest surviving detailed account of royal revenues, the pipe roll of 1129–30, shows just how lucrative patronage could be. In this financial year Henry I is recorded as having collected about £3,600 from agreements of this kind. This is about 15 per cent of his recorded revenue and more than he got from taxation. But the arithmetic of the pipe roll tells us a good deal more than this. In 1129–30 the total sum due as a result of agreements made in this and previous years was almost £26,000, that is only 14 per cent of the amount due was actually collected. William de Pont de l'Arche, for example, had offered 1,000 marks for a chamberlainship and in 1129–30 he paid 100 marks. This meant that if the king were satisfied with William's behaviour, then payment of further instalments might be suspended or pardoned. The expectation that the exchequer would not press too hard had the effect of encouraging men to bid highly. But a man who fell out of favour would find that he had to pay up promptly—or get into even worse trouble. This, for example, was the fate which befell William de Braose in John's reign. In other words, collecting only a small proportion of the amount due was not an indication of chronic government inefficiency but rather of a further refinement of an infinitely flexible system of patronage.

Masterful kings always had their hands in their subjects' pockets. Edward I was known as *Le Roi Coveytous* just as William I had 'loved greediness above all'. At a more abstract level, as early as the twelfth century it was asserted that royal power can be measured in financial terms. In the words of Richard FitzNeal, bishop of London, Treasurer of England, and author of *The Dialogue of the Exchequer*, a work dating from the 1170s, 'the power of princes fluctuates according to the ebb and flow of their cash resources'. The pipe roll of 1129–30—a record of the accounts presented at the exchequer by sheriffs and other officials in that year—shows an exchequer system already working very much along the lines described in *The Dialogue*. But the financial system itself certainly pre-dated the pipe roll. In broad outline—annual renders made by sheriffs to the treasury—it is an Anglo-Saxon system. In 1066 and 1086 the renders produced by some large royal manors were still paid in kind. By 1129–30 it is clear that a widespread commutation into money rents had taken place. This was in line with general European development. The more the sheriffs' renders were made in cash, the greater the need for an easily followed but quick method of making calculations in pounds, shillings, and pence. Thus the chequered table cloth (from which the word exchequer is derived) served as a simplified abacus, on which the king's *calculator* did sums by moving counters from square to square like a croupier. The earliest reference to the exchequer dates from 1110. Twice a year a group of the most powerful and trusted men in the realm met in order to audit the sheriffs' accounts. When the king was in Normandy they would meet, as the vice-regal committee 'at the exchequer', in the king's absence. Presumably a similarly composed committee had met for a similar purpose when Cnut was in Denmark.

But this is speculation. It is only when we reach 1129–30 that some degree of precision is possible. Even here, however, we have to be careful. An exchequer record, a pipe roll, tells almost nothing about those sums which were paid into and out of the chamber. Certainly these sums cannot be quantified, though in view of the fact that the chamber was the financial office of the itinerant household it is likely that they were large. For example it was estimated that by 1187 Henry II had paid 30,000 marks into his Jerusalem bank account though there is no sign of this money in the pipe rolls of his reign. In the absence of twelfth-century chamber records, it is not easy to estimate total royal revenue. Thus, the low pipe roll totals in

the early years of Henry II's reign may be very largely a reflec-
tion of the new king's preference for chamber finance, a very
natural preference for an Angevin prince, all of whose fore-
fathers had managed perfectly well without an exchequer. After
all, when it came to minting coins the Angevins introduced
Angevin practice into both England and Normandy. But, whatever the difficulties, analysis of the only surviving pipe roll of
Henry I's reign is undoubtedly revealing.

In 1129–30, £22,865 was paid into the treasury. Out of this
total almost £12,000 comes under the heading of 'land and
associated profits'. Just under £3,000 can be described as taxation, nearly all of this (almost £2,500) being Danegeld, as the
geld (see p. 168) was commonly called in the twelfth century.
Another £7,200 can be described as the profits of feudal
lordship and jurisdiction: this included about £1,000 from
ecclesiastical vacancies; £2,400 from judicial fines; and the
£3,600 from agreements mentioned earlier. Thus over half the
recorded revenue came from land; about a third from lordship
and jurisdiction; and only some 13 per cent from taxation. If
we compare this with the state of royal revenues in the early
years of Edward I's reign then some significant differences
emerge. In very rough terms, land accounted for about a third
of the total; lordship and jurisdiction may well have provided
less than 10 per cent, while taxation (including customs duties)
accounted for over a half. Land, lordship, and jurisdiction
became relatively less important; taxation became much more
important. Even allowing for the likelihood that tax revenue in
1129–30 was rather less than usual (because the geld was the
only tax levied that year), this broad generalization would still
hold.

Though the royal lands were immensely lucrative in 1130, a
comparison with Domesday Book suggests that they were
already a declining asset. In 1086 the total recorded value of the
king's lands and boroughs was almost £14,000, while by 1129–
30 it had gone down to less than £10,700. It seems that the
stock of royal lands was dwindling faster than it was being

replenished by forfeitures and reversions to the Crown (escheats). Kings had to grant land to powerful men. They did so in order to reward and encourage loyalty, particularly early in their reigns when faced with the problems of disputed succession. This process continued, but was to some extent offset by attempts to manage the royal estates more efficiently. The success of these managerial reforms, begun under Hubert Walter, then continued by John's and Henry III's ministers, can be measured by the fact that Edward I was still able to enjoy a revenue from land of some £13,000 a year. (In view of the inflation in the previous one hundred and fifty years, however, this means that real income from this source was a good deal less than it had been in 1129–30. Equally £20,000 under Henry I was probably worth more than £40,000 under Edward I.)

The geld, the hide—the unit of land on which the geld was assessed—and the fiscal machinery through which the geld was collected, are all further examples of those rights which the Norman kings inherited from the Anglo-Saxons. Even though at two shillings on the hide the geld contributed only 10 per cent of Henry I's recorded income, it was clearly a valuable royal asset. By 1129–30 it had become an annual tax and one which could occasionally be levied at a higher rate (moreover geld exemptions could be granted as political favours, adding yet another string to the bow of royal patronage). But the geld was levied only twice by Henry II, in 1155–6 and 1161–2. Instead he developed other levies, the aid of knights (scutage: assessed on knights' fees) and the aid of boroughs and cities (tallage: assessed on a valuation of movable property). By John's reign, scutages and tallages between them constituted a more or less annual tax which adequately compensated the Crown for the withering away of the geld. But the geld was not quite dead. Under a new name, carucage, and a revised assessment it was revived and levied four times between 1194 and 1220.

By this date, however, the government had discovered a new and altogether more productive form of tax, assessed not on land but on an estimate of a man's revenues and movable property. Probably based on the ecclesiastical tithe, it was initially used in 1166, 1185, and 1188 for a pious purpose—the financial support of the Holy Land. John certainly levied this tax on movables in 1207, and may have done so in 1203. An account of the 1207 tax survives and the figures which it discloses are astonishing. Levied at the rate of $\frac{1}{13}$ it produced no less than £60,000—a sum far and away in excess of the yield of other taxes. (Yet in 1194 this same tax had been levied at the rate of $\frac{1}{4}$—the heaviest rate in the long history of the tax—in order to contribute to Richard's ransom). In the mid-1190s the first national customs system was introduced. These developments suggest that royal revenues reached new high levels during Richard's and John's reign. By 1213–14 John had accumulated some 200,000 marks. But these large accumulations were soon spent. These were years of war, of the Third Crusade and of the defence of the Angevin Empire. John's final failure in 1214 ushered in a long period of relative peace. Not until 1294 would the English taxpayer once again find himself paying for a major European war.

In the mean time, however, there were two other significant thirteenth-century innovations—the development of taxation of the clergy, and the establishment of a customs system. Since 1199 the Church had been made subject to an income tax imposed by the pope. Initially intended to finance crusades, it was later used for a variety of 'good causes'—as defined by the pope. Thus in 1217 Honorius III ordered bishops and prelates to help out the boy-king Henry III. From then on the Church was frequently required to subsidize the king, particularly if he had taken the cross, as Henry III did in 1250 and Edward I did in 1287. In 1291, for example, Edward received no less than 100,000 marks out of the proceeds of a papal crusading tax. By the mid-thirteenth century it had already become clear that the English Church was prepared to give financial aid to the king—though, naturally, assemblies of clergy haggled over the amount and took the opportunity of their meeting to discuss other matters which they felt needed remedying. Hardly surprising then that Henry III should go one step further in 1254 and ask for a clerical grant without first seeking papal consent. This precedent was followed in 1269, and then on three occasions by Edward I (1279/80, 1283, and 1290) in the years before 1294.

The customs duty in Richard's and John's reigns had been a war measure; it lapsed when John sought a truce with Philip Augustus in 1206. The importance of the duty on wool exports established in 1275 was that it became a permanent addition to the Crown's peacetime revenue. Its yield varied according to the fortunes of the wool trade but at the rate agreed in 1275, half a mark (6s. 8d.) per sack, it brought in between £8,000 and £13,000 per annum in the years before 1294. These new measures, papal taxation of the English Church and the customs duty on wool, were both related to the presence of Italian mercantile and banking houses in England. On the one hand, it was the ubiquitous Italian businessman that enabled the thirteenth-century Papacy to operate as an international finance corporation. On the other, credit finance came to play an increasingly large part in government. Edward I's debt to the Ricciardi of Lucca for the years from 1272 to 1294 totalled nearly £400,000; 48 per cent of this debt was repaid out of the customs receipt from a trade in which the Italians were increasingly involved. Kings, of course, had borrowed before. In the 1250s, Henry III owed the Ricciardi over £50,000; in the 1150s, Henry II used loans from a Flemish businessman, William Cade, to finance the making of the Angevin Empire. What was significant in the late thirteenth century was both the scale of the operations and the linkage between credit and customs. Compared with the sums obtainable from these new sources, the amounts to be derived from traditional levies, scutages, tallages, and feudal aids, were hardly worth the trouble of collecting and they gradually fell into disuse.

The customs system of 1275 had been granted in Parliament after discussion between the king's advisers and the merchants. Characteristic of all these taxes was that someone else's consent was required: either the pope's, or the merchants', or the clergy's, or the country's. By contrast land, lordship, and juris- diction were revenue-producing rights which did not require meetings of influential men to approve their exploitation— indeed all influential men enjoyed similar rights (though on a smaller scale) and presumably took them for granted—so long as they were not abused. Whereas 85 per cent of Henry I's recorded revenue came from land, lordship, and jurisdiction, they provided less than 40 per cent of Edward I's. The higher the proportion of Crown revenue that came from taxation, the greater was the need for political mechanisms that enabled that consent to be obtained. This is the process known as the growth of representative institutions; in the case of the tax on movables it is the growth of Parliament.

During the long years of freedom from foreign war after 1214 the tax on movables remained an occasional resource of the Crown. War was occasional and other acceptable justifica- tions for the tax were rare, so consent was only occasionally forthcoming—certainly not as often as Henry III would have liked. But the growing potential of the tax was revealed by the last of the seven levies collected between 1208 and 1293: the assessed yield of the $\frac{1}{15}$ of 1290 was over £116,000. How was consent to this extraordinary tax obtained? The king's advisers would have had to make a case. Presumably, they pointed to the expenses of his recent stay in Gascony (1286–9) and of his future crusade; they may well have pointed out that in the interests of Christian piety he was sacrificing a lucrative source of revenue in deciding to expel the Jews—although by 1290 the Jewish community had been squeezed so hard by royal financial demands that it had little more to give. But to whom did they make the case? They made it to the men who represented 'the community of the realm' and, in the first instance, these were the magnates—the sorts of influential men who always had attended major political assemblies, whether Anglo-Saxon, Norman, or Angevin. The assembly of 1290, 'Parliament' as it was now called, met from April to July and in its first ten weeks

it got through a great deal of business, including some important legislation. In mid-July another group of men arrived,
knights of the shire. Less than a week later Parliament was
dissolved. Why had the knights been so belatedly summoned to
attend? Because the magnates were reluctant to approve the
tax. They agreed to it but 'only insofar as they were entitled to'.
Yet they had not been similarly reluctant to deal with other
kinds of parliamentary business, judicial, political, legislative.
In other words the magnates still adequately represented 'the
community of the realm' in most fields—but not when taxation
was on the agenda. From the late twelfth century onwards,
kings had grown accustomed to bargaining with individual
shire communities, so it was an obvious step to require these
local communities to choose men to speak for them on some of
those occasions when the king wanted to summon an assembly
to represent the community of the whole realm. Assemblies of
magnates were being reinforced in this way from the 1250s
onwards and gradually the knights, yeomen, and burgesses who
represented shires and boroughs—the Commons—were being
accorded a more prominent role. As the proceedings of the
Parliament of 1290 make clear it was above all else the king's
need for taxation which stimulated this development.

Was the process also the result of social change? Was there a
thirteenth-century 'rise of the gentry' which meant that traditional political institutions had to be reshaped? Did the gentry
now count for more in the localities so that if kings wanted
their needs widely understood and their taxes efficiently collected they had to offer them a place in the main political
forum of the realm? These are difficult questions, so difficult
indeed to answer in the affirmative that some historians have
argued that, on the contrary, the thirteenth century was a
period of crisis for the knightly class. One of the problems is a
familiar one: the growing volume of evidence. We know much
more about the thirteenth-century gentry than we do about
their predecessors. But did Simon de Montfort and his friends
court the gentry more assiduously in the period 1258–65 than

John and the rebel barons had done in 1212–15? Magna Carta contains clauses which appeal to wider social groups than the barons, but so too does Henry I's Coronation Charter. To whom was Edward the Confessor appealing when, in 1051, he decided not to collect the *heregeld*? Neither in the twelfth century nor in Anglo-Saxon times did society consist only of barons and peasants. The sort of men who got themselves chosen to be knights of the shire in the late thirteenth century were exactly the sort of men who always had attended the great political assemblies. True, they had come then in the retinues of the magnates, but it was in their retinues that sensible magnates found their best advisers—and presumably they had listened to them. The knights of the late thirteenth century were not coming to these meetings for the first time; they were simply coming under another guise. It may be that the evidence of political change—the more elaborate representative institutions of the thirteenth century, the larger share of taxation in crown revenue—still has to be set within a framework of underlying social continuity.

Law and Justice

From the reign of Henry II onwards, royal judges began to hold local sessions (assizes) so frequently that it becomes possible to speak of the application over almost the entire country of a common body of customary law, the 'common law', the custom of the king's court as described in treatises such as 'Glanvill' and 'Bracton'. The previous system had been one in which, generally speaking, local courts had applied local custom. Kings, of course, had long been held to be responsible for law and order; in particular they were expected to deal with serious offences, the pleas of the Crown, but until a regular, centrally-directed machinery of justice was established, their activity in this field could only be sporadic. They intervened when influential people were involved and they launched occasional drives against theft, especially cattle-rustling. In this respect, the

Anglo-Saxon system of justice survived the Norman Conquest. The change came in 1166 with the Assize of Clarendon, reinforced in 1176 by the Assize of Northampton. These assizes introduced regular measures for the trial by royal judges of those suspected of serious crimes. At first Henry II's judges were simply men whom the king trusted—they might be earls, barons, bishops, abbots, or counsellors from the royal household, exactly the sort of people whom earlier kings had sent out on specific commissions of justice or inquiry—the biggest and most famous of such inquiries being the Domesday survey. For men such as these, holding courts of law was just one of the many tasks, administrative, diplomatic, and military, which they carried out on the king's behalf. But the introduction of frequent circuits meant an ever-increasing burden of judicial work and by the end of the twelfth century we can identify a group of men, most of them laymen, who specialized in legal business, in effect professional judges. There were, of course, lower courts dealing with less serious offences, but the 'professional' courts increasingly came to dominate the field. For one thing the lower courts had no authority to innovate, whereas the king could, and did, create new offences. For example the crime of conspiracy was 'invented' in 1279 when Edward I ordered the itinerant judges to inquire into confederacies to defeat the ends of justice. Since the king's courts dealt not only with crime but also with disputes concerning property they were clearly felt to be performing a useful service. Magna Carta criticized many aspects of royal government, but not this one. Indeed it asked that the king's judges should visit each shire four times a year, more frequently than was in practice possible.

The judges were men learned in the law; being learned, they naturally responded to shifts in attitudes and ideas prevailing within educated opinion. One such shift was in the direction of a self-consciously rational approach to intellectual problems—an approach typified by Abelard's dictum: 'By doubting we come to inquiry, by inquiring we come to perceive the truth.'

When applied to the law, this was a dictum which could have far-reaching implications. For example, if the guilt or innocence of a suspect could not readily be determined, it had for centuries been customary to send him to the ordeal, usually the ordeal of hot iron or the ordeal of water. This system worked well enough while men believed in it—it relied on the same psychological insight as the modern lie-detector—but was highly vulnerable to doubt. If an innocent man came to doubt the ordeal's efficacy as the means whereby God would prove his innocence then he was all the more likely to fail the ordeal. Once raised, these doubts could not be stilled. At first they seemed shocking—as when voiced by William Rufus—but eventually they became conventional. Finally, in 1215 Pope Innocent III forbade the participation of priests in the ordeal and, in England at least, this meant that the system came to an abrupt end. After an initial period of confusion, trial by ordeal was replaced by trial by jury: this was a method which had already been used with some success in settling disputes about possession of land. In 1179 Henry II had ordered that, in a case concerning property rights, the defendant might opt for trial by jury rather than trial by battle—the method which had been introduced into England by the Normans and the efficacy of which, like the ordeal, was vulnerable to doubt. But this rule when applied to criminal justice meant that there was a trial only when the accused opted for one. Obviously he came under great pressure. By a statute of 1275 he was condemned to a 'prisone forte et dure' until he did opt for trial. In consequence, many men died in prison, but because they had not been convicted, their property was not forfeited to the Crown. For this reason some chose to die rather than risk trial. Not until the eighteenth century was this right to choose taken away.

At first, and particularly in property litigation, juries had been called upon to settle straightforward questions to which they might reasonably be expected to know the answer. But problems arose when more complicated cases came before them and when trial by jury replaced the ordeal. For, unlike God, a jury was not omniscient. So efforts were made to cut through the complexities of any given dispute in order to isolate a specific question which the jury could fairly be expected to decide. But to do this well required specialized knowledge and skill; in other words it needed professional lawyers. And so, in the course of the thirteenth century, a legal profession developed, with its own schools, its own literature, and its own language (law French).

Despite all these changes, in many fundamental respects Anglo-Saxon attitudes towards justice continued to flourish. In the Anglo-Saxon and Anglo-Norman periods, serious offences had been dealt with under a procedure which ended with the guilty party being required to pay compensation to the victim or his family. The new machinery of justice established by the Angevins tended to impose punishment without compensation. In many cases, homicide, wounding, and rape for example, this was felt to be intolerable, so despite the impression given by writers such as 'Glanvill' and 'Bracton' who would have us believe that the new principles had effectively displaced the old, it seems that in reality the old procedures survived; they were adapted and grafted on to the new. What this meant was that those who could afford it escaped punishment but paid compensation to the victim or his kin, while those who could not, suffered the consequences.

Church and Religion

Domesday Book suggests that the village priest was usually reckoned to be a member of the peasant community. His church belonged to the local lord. If an estate were divided then the profits of the church which went with that estate might also have to be divided. In many ways, the village priest shared the life-style of the ordinary villager. He was very unlikely to be celibate; indeed, he was probably married and may well have inherited his position from his father. Given this basic situation, one can only admire the temerity of those eleventh-century reformers who aimed to abolish both lay control of the Church and the family life of the clergy. Under papal stimulus, the campaign for reform reached England in 1076. In subsequent decades, it was gradually stepped up and in the long run it even had a kind of success. By the late thirteenth century, married clergy were exceptional. On the other hand, plenty of them—including some of the most powerful—continued to have mistresses. Ranulf Flambard of Durham and Roger of Salisbury had their counterparts almost two hundred years later in Walter Langton of Coventry, who was accused of strangling his mistress's husband, and Robert Burnell, Edward I's chancellor, whom the king twice tried to have translated from Bath and Wells to Canterbury. As far as lay patronage and family connection were concerned, these two aspects of church life were hardly touched. 'The Lord deprived bishops of sons, but the devil gave them nephews.'

Yet even the limited success of the campaign against clerical marriage is remarkable—given how ineffective decrees on this subject had been in the seven hundred years from the fourth century onwards. It may well be linked with the general improvement in education in the twelfth and thirteenth centuries. If society at large became more literate then the clergy could more readily be recruited from the laity; they did not have to remain what they had come close to being, a hereditary caste. The more people went to school, the more they learned to know, and some of them to respect, the ancient law of the Church. Certainly there is reason to believe that in thirteenth-century England a higher proportion of the population was celibate than had been in the eleventh century. Quite simply, there were far more people who had taken vows of chastity. Everywhere in Europe monasticism flourished and England was no exception. In 1066 there were some fifty religious houses in England and perhaps 1,000 monks and nuns. By 1216 there were approximately 700 houses and some 13,000 monks, nuns, canons, and canonesses. A century later, the total was nearer 900 houses and 17,500 members of the religious orders. Seen in the context of an overall tripling of the population these are impressive figures. Even so they fail to make plain the extent to which religious life had become diversified and enriched. In the eleventh century, all the houses were Benedictine in type. By the mid-thirteenth century not only were there several hundred Benedictine houses, there were also a number of new orders from which a man or woman could choose—regular canons, Cistercians, Gilbertines (the one peculiarly English order), Templars, Hospitallers, Carthusians, Dominicans, Franciscans, Carmelites, and Austin friars. Within this framework, almost every conceivable variety of religious life, rural, urban, contemplative, ascetic, active, was now catered for. What is more, most of those who entered the religious life now did so because they chose to. Whereas the old Benedictine houses had recruited their monks largely from the children given by their aristocratic parents to be brought up in the cloister (oblates), from the mid-twelfth century onwards those who entered both the new and the old orders were adults. The Cistercians, who established the new pattern, prohibited entry for anyone under the age of sixteen and insisted upon a year's noviciate. Conscripts had been replaced by volunteers.

During the course of the twelfth century, the English Church established the diocesan and parochial organization under which it was to live for centuries. The last new dioceses to be created were Ely (in 1108) and Carlisle (1133). Dioceses were divided into archdeaconries, and archdeaconries into rural deaneries. In the Norman period, as before, new parishes were created almost at will—the will of the local lord; but thereafter it became much harder. The territorial organization of the Church became, as it were, frozen in its twelfth-century state. This was certainly not because demographic and economic expansion was now levelling off. On the contrary, new settlements continued to be founded and the old ones continued to grow. What was happening was that the development of canon law and of papal jurisdiction was tending to protect innumerable vested interests. The rise of the lawyer, itself the result of change in one sphere of life, made it harder to change things in others. Where this created a real pastoral problem was in the towns. Bishops wrestled with the problem but much of their effort was frustrated by the proprietary interests of patrons, churchmen as well as laymen. The thirteenth century found a solution, but it needed a radical departure, a new form of religious life, to make it possible. This new form was provided by the mendicant orders, the friars—mobile missionaries whose international organization cut clean through diocesan and parochial boundaries. The first friars to come to England were the Dominicans. They arrived in 1221 and headed for Oxford. Three years later, the Franciscans arrived; their earliest friaries were in Canterbury, London, and Oxford. The Carmelites and Austin friars arrived in the 1240s. By 1300 the friars had founded some 150 houses in England.

The coming of the friars, like the growth of canon law, is a movement which reflects one of the basic circumstances of the English Church. Although its growing material wealth was firmly rooted in English soil, in its spiritual, intellectual, and corporate life as a Church it was simply a part of Latin Christendom. This was particularly true of the period from the late eleventh century onwards. Even though the Anglo-Saxon Church had always been open to Continental influences, the fact that, after 1066, it became French in its speech and emphatically Latin in its learning tended to accentuate this receptiveness. Still more important was the Gregorian reform movement and the associated development of canon law and papal jurisdiction over the entire Latin Church. The reformers' demand for *libertas ecclesiae*, the privileged freedom of the Church, undeniably had some dramatic consequences; but in the end it turned out to be unobtainable. While liberty was linked with privilege and the continued possession of great corporate wealth, kings and other secular patrons could not afford to renounce some of their crucial powers, in particular the power to appoint, even though by the thirteenth century they were having to work through the legal machinery of the Roman curia in order to obtain their ends. The fact was that the spiritual weapons at the Church's disposal, excommunication and interdict, were ultimately insufficient to deter the secular power. They tended, moreover, to become blunted through over-use. In areas which really mattered to the lay world, not just patronage but also war, tournaments, and business practice, the heroic days of the Gregorian reform gradually, in the course of the twelfth and thirteenth centuries, gave way to a period of accommodation. But where the reformers did succeed was in translating the theory of papal headship of the Church into the fact of a centralized system of government. To a quite remarkable extent, the clergy learned to do what the pope told them to do. Thus when Pope Innocent III, in pursuit of his quarrel with King John, laid an interdict on England, the clergy obeyed. For six years, from 1208 to 1214, the church doors were closed and the laity were locked out; they were denied the sacrament of the altar, solemnization of marriages, burial in consecrated ground. Even when the pope, beginning in 1199, ordered the taxation of the Church, the clergy grumbled but paid up. From 1228 onwards we can trace a continuous series of resident collectors in England; they bore the title of *nuncio* and almost all of them were Italians. Here too there was accommodation. It seemed realistic to win the king of England's approval and so, by 1300, it was the king who received the lion's share of the proceeds.

Throughout this period, Catholic Christianity remained the unchallenged religion of the country. It was taken for granted. When the churches were closed for six years there was hardly a murmur of public protest—but neither was there an upsurge of interest in alternative religions. In the twelfth and thirteenth centuries, heresy was no more of a threat to the English Church than it had been in the eleventh: in this respect England was different from many parts of Europe. Throughout this period there were a few non-Christians—Jews—in the country, but their position was always precarious, at times painfully so, and in 1290 they were expelled. Most Christians rejoiced.

Economy

The basic outline of the English economy in 1086 emerges very clearly from the repetitive, laconic phrases of Domesday Book. This was a fundamentally agrarian economy. Over 90 per cent of the people lived in the country and earned their daily bread and ale from the resources of the land. The land was already well settled—some 13,000 settlements are named—and much cultivated. As much as 80 per cent of the arable acreage of 1914 had been under the plough in 1086. Pasture, woodland, and fen were also exploited. Most men were farmers and fishers. Neither trade nor industry could offer a major alternative source of employment. Domesday statistics—though they have to be used as cautiously as any other statistics—can help to fill out the picture. People called *villani* comprised the most numerous class (41 per cent of the total recorded population). Their land holdings came to about 45 per cent of all the land. The next largest number (32 per cent) were the people known as 'bordars' or 'cottars'; they held only 5 per cent of the land. Thus, although there were enormous individual variations, it is clear that we are dealing with two distinct classes: those who had a substantial stake in the village fields and those who possessed hardly more than a cottage and its garden. In addition there were the 14 per cent of the total who were described either as 'free men' or 'sokemen'. Since they held a fifth of the land they seem to belong, economically speaking, to the same class as the *villani*. Finally there were the slaves, 9 per cent of the recorded population, who held no land.

At the other end of the social scale were the king and a tiny group of powerful men, all of them *rentiers* who lived in style on the revenues of their great estates. Less than two hundred laymen and roughly one hundred major churches (bishoprics, abbeys, and priories) held between them about three-quarters of the assessed value of the whole country. These men—in legal terminology they were known as the king's tenants-in-chief—had tenants of their own. A wealthy baron like William de

Warenne, for example, had granted out holdings worth about £540 out of an estate valued at over £1,150. Some of these subtenants were men described as knights and their tenancies as knights' fees. (Although many of the knights were no richer than the richest *villani* the fact remains that they lived in closer association with their lords and therefore belonged to a different social group.) The rest of a tenant-in-chief's estates— usually between a half and three-quarters of them—were kept 'in demesne', and it was from these demesne lands that a lord drew the bulk of his income and food. A monastic house, with a fixed centre, needed regular supplies of foodstuffs, but other great landlords, who were more peripatetic, would probably be more interested in money. Most demesnes therefore were leased—'farmed' was the technical term—in return for a money rent. Most of the lessees came from exactly the same range of social ranks as did the holders of knights' fees; together they constituted a landowning 'middle class', a gentry.

What happened to the English economy in the two hundred years after 1086? Even over so long a period as this it can be argued that, in many fundamental respects, there was little change. England was no more urbanized in 1286 than in 1086. True, there were more and larger towns but then there were more people altogether. There were undoubtedly striking improvements in ship design—a continuing feature of northern Europe from the eighth century onwards. In this period it meant, above all, the development of the 'cog', a large, tubby bulk-carrier with a stern-post rudder and a deep draught. This meant economies of scale in the maritime trade which had long linked the east coast with the Scandinavian world and the west with the Atlantic coast of France. Presumably the volume of trade in wool, cloth, timber, salted fish, and wine was increasing and merchants' profits may well have been increasing too. Even so there was no English commercial revolution, no development of banks and credit facilities of the kind that can be claimed for thirteenth-century Italy. One consequence of this relative backwardness was that in the thirteenth century an increasingly high proportion of England's foreign trade came to be in Italian hands. Their reserves of liquid capital enabled Italian companies to offer attractive terms. They could not only buy an abbey's entire wool clip for the current year; they could also buy it for years in advance. By lending large sums to Henry III and Edward I, they obtained royal patronage and protection. In a very real sense late thirteenth-century England was being treated as a partially developed economy. Much of its import–export business was handled by foreigners (Gascons and Flemings as well as Italians). Its main exports were raw materials—wool and grain—rather than manufactured goods. There had been, in other words, no industrial revolution.

Throughout this period the major industries remained the same ones: cloth, building, mining and metalworking, salt production, and sea fishing. Moreover, despite the claims sometimes made for the cloth fulling-mill, there were no significant advances in industrial technology. Nor was there anything to compare with the highly-capitalized development of the Flemish cloth industry in the twelfth and thirteenth centuries. On the other hand growing Flemish demand for English wool did help to preserve the favourable balance of trade which, throughout this period, ensured an inflow of bullion sufficient to maintain the one coin, the silver penny, at a consistently fine standard. (Whereas in more rapidly developing and more highly monetized regions, people used a much debased coinage to perform the economic function of small change. In this sense too the English economy saw comparatively little change.)

Above all there was no agricultural revolution. Despite the fact that thirteenth-century experts on estate management, men such as Walter of Henley or Henry of Eastry, approached their job in a rational and scientific manner, the technical limitations under which they worked meant that no significant increase in yields was possible, neither from sheep in terms of weight of fleece, nor from seed in terms of yield of grain. Though the use of the horse as a draught animal was spreading, this was of marginal importance. The main problems lay not in ploughing, but in sowing, reaping, and maintaining soil fertility. Sowing and reaping by hand was wasteful and slow. Marl and most other types of fertilizer were either expensive or unobtainable. Only animal dung was generally available and it was widely and systematically used. But the high costs of feeding flocks and herds through the winter meant that there were upper limits to the amount of dung that could be produced. And unless there were basic improvements in primary production—as there were not—improvements at the second stage of production, for example the introduction of windmills around 1200, could only be of marginal economic importance. Thus in many respects England remained a stagnant economy. It can indeed be argued that, by comparison with some of its neighbours, especially Flanders and Italy, England was less advanced in the thirteenth century than it had been in the eleventh.

But having said all this, it must be made clear that in one vital respect there had been considerable change. By the late thirteenth century there were far more people living in England than there had been in 1086—notwithstanding the fact that men and women were familiar with *coitus interruptus* as a method of birth control. Exactly how many people there were, it is impossible to say. Estimating population at the time of the Domesday survey is an extremely difficult task. Most historians would put it at between one and a quarter and two and a quarter millions. Estimating the late thirteenth-century population is even more hazardous. Some historians would go as high as seven millions; others would put it much lower, perhaps five millions. But almost all agree that the population more than doubled and most would accept that it probably trebled. The hypothesis of slow growth from the eleventh (or perhaps indeed from the tenth) century, followed by an acceleration from the end of the twelfth century onwards seems to be a plausible one. But not only did rates of growth vary (probably) over time; they also varied (certainly) in space. Thus the population of the

North Riding of Yorkshire probably increased some twelvefold in the two hundred years after 1086; elsewhere, and particularly in those areas which were already relatively densely settled by the time of the Domesday survey, that is along the south coast and in some parts of East Anglia, the growth rate was very much smaller, though it was particularly high in the silt belt around the Wash.

What were the economic consequences of this increase of population? They can best be summed up by the phrase, 'expansion without growth'. Thus the immediate consequence was the physical expansion of settlement and cultivation. The expansion of settlement was a fairly straightforward matter. Indeed, there are plenty of signs of what the citizen of the modern world is inclined to call progress. Towns flourished. Their main function was to act as local markets. Where we know the occupations of their inhabitants, the predominance of the victualling trades and of craftsmen-shopkeepers in leather, metal, and textiles is striking. Even for the big towns—and by European standards England contained only one genuinely big town, London, assessed in 1334 at four times the wealth of its nearest rival, Bristol—long-distance and luxury trade remained less important. An increasing density of rural population meant that towns increased both in size and in number. Between 1100 and 1300, some 140 new towns were planted and, if it is not just a trick of the evidence, it would seem that the decades between 1170 and 1250 saw the greatest number, Portsmouth, Leeds, Liverpool, Chelmsford, Salisbury, for example. Mostly they were founded by local lords who expected to make a profit out of the money rents and tolls they planned to collect. Some were sited where they could take advantage of the expansion of maritime commerce, as larger ships meant that coastal ports such as Boston, King's Lynn, and Hull (all new foundations) did better than up-river ports such as Lincoln, Norwich, and York.

In the countryside, too, the hand of the planner is sometimes visible, particularly in the regular-form villages which were laid out in those northern areas which had been laid waste by the Normans. Elsewhere, in already densely settled East Anglia for example, villages sometimes moved to new sites straggling along the edge of common land, presumably in order to free good arable land from the 'waste' of being built upon.

But finding room to live was one thing; growing enough food to live on quite another. In general the expansion of farmland took place not so much through the establishment of new settlements as through piecemeal increase around existing centres. Huge acreages of forest, fen, marsh, and upland were cleared, drained, and farmed. Some of this was on potentially good soil—the silt belt around the Wash is the classic example—but much of it, like the clearings in the Sussex Weald, would always remain poor. This is 'the journey to the margin'—men moved out to the margins of cultivation and farmed land that was indeed marginal: it produced returns which were barely worth the labour expended. So pressing was the demand for food, bread above all, that even other 'necessities'—fuel and building timber—were having to give way.

Naturally attempts were made to farm the existing arable more intensively. In the thirteenth century the three-field, instead of the two-field, system came to be more widely adopted. This meant that a third rather than a half of the land was left fallow each year. But more intensive land use required a correspondingly more intensive application of fertilizers if soil quality were to be maintained. Unfortunately, the expansion of arable was sometimes at the expense of both pasture and woodland. The effect of this on livestock numbers could hardly have permitted increased manure production and may have actually led to a decrease in droppings. This in turn could have led to soil exhaustion and lower, rather than higher yields. Whether or not yields did decline towards the end of the thirteenth century, one thing that does seem clear is that, if the physical limit of cultivation were reached and population still continued to grow, then one of two things would have to happen.

Either more food would be imported or the average standard of living would have to fall. There is no evidence that grain imports rose. If anything the trend was probably in the opposite direction. English grain dealers took their merchandise in bulk-carrying ships to regions such as Flanders, Gascony, and Norway, that is, to places where industrialization or specialization had reached a higher pitch than in England and where regional economies were geared to the import of basic foodstuffs in return for cloth, wine, and forest products. Moreover the abundant estate records of thirteenth-century England make it clear that the average size of tenant holdings was shrinking. In this period more people means less land per head.

Despite this gloomy picture many thirteenth-century villagers may have been better off than their predecessors at the time of Domesday Book. They were relatively free from the devastation caused by war. None of them was a slave. Slavery is a feature of economies characterized by labour shortage; as population, and therefore the supply of labour, rose so slavery declined. True, many of them were serfs (or villeins)—perhaps as much as half the total population—whereas the *villani* and cottagers of Domesday Book (three-quarters of the listed population) were free. But although the *villani* and cottagers were free inasmuch as they were not slaves, it is clear that they were not very free—thus the existence of the much smaller Domesday class (only 14 per cent of those listed) called precisely 'free men'. What made life difficult for the *villani* and cottagers was that their lords were free too—free and powerful. They were free to manipulate custom in order to impose as many burdens as they could, and in a period of relative labour shortage this is likely to have meant a heavy regime of labour services: at times like this lords would not be content to pay wages at levels set by the market. Only as supply rose would lords increasingly turn to the alternative of wage labour. In the twelfth century, many tenants found their obligations converted from labour service to payment of a money rent. At this point, the development of the legalistic outlook becomes important. In the decades either side of the year 1200, the king's judges formulated rules to determine who had the right to have their disputes heard in the royal courts and who had not. They decided that those who had the right were 'free', while those who had not were 'servile'. The effect of this classification of society into two distinct categories was to enserf half the population: to make them legally unfree. But what the lawyers took with one hand they gave with the other. The more everything came to be defined and written down, the more customary tenures tended to become 'frozen' in that state in which they were written down. It became less easy to manipulate custom; more effectively than before custom tended to protect the status quo. In this sense, even unfree tenants in the thirteenth century were less vulnerable to the arbitrary exactions of individual lords than many free tenants of the eleventh century had been. Thirteenth-century lords who tried to manipulate custom often found themselves involved in long legal battles with well-organized village communities.

But although customary law may have offered a poor tenant some protection from his lord's demands, it could do nothing to protect him from the grim realities of economic change. In the years either side of 1200, half the villagers of England may have been enserfed, but this mattered little compared with the fact that poor villagers became still poorer. Those who really suffered towards the end of the thirteenth century were not servile tenants as such, but those tenants, whether free or servile, who were poor and those who had no land at all. We know something about tenants. Mortality rates on the Winchester manors suggest that from 1250 onwards the poorer tenants were becoming increasingly 'harvest-sensitive'—a euphemistic phrase meaning that, with each bad harvest, more of them died, either of starvation or of the diseases attendant upon malnutrition. Study of the West Midlands manor of Halesowen suggests that poor tenants there—the successors of the cottagers of Domesday—had a life expectancy some ten years less than the better-off tenants, the successors of the Domesday *villani*. What happened to the landless we can only guess; the nature of the evidence is such that they rarely find themselves mentioned in thirteenth-century records. Labourers on great estates customarily received not only cash but also an allowance of grain sufficient to sustain a family. But what about those landless labourers who became 'surplus to the economy'? Presumably they also became 'harvest-sensitive'.

But the economic clouds which brought misery for the poor were nicely lined with silver for the rich. The growth of population meant an increasing demand for food. Prices rose, particularly around 1200 and in the late thirteenth-century. On the other hand, a plentiful supply of labour meant that money wage rates, both for piece-work and for day-work, remained stable throughout the century. Real wages, in other words, fell. In these circumstances, wealthy landowners could do very well. Selling their surplus produce on the market brought increasing profits. Markets proliferated. Between 1198 and 1483 some 2,400 grants of market were made by the Crown and of these over half came in the period before 1275. Equally a rising demand for tenancies meant growing rent-rolls. To take just one example, the bishop of Ely's net income rose from £920 in 1171-2 to £2,550 in 1298. But this does not quite mean that all the fortunate possessor of a great estate had to do was sit back and let the laws of supply and demand do their work for him. In the twelfth century, as before, most of the manors belonging to a wealthy tenant-in-chief were in fact held by his tenants, either as knights' fees or leased out at fixed rents to 'farmers'. At a time of stability or gradual expansion, this made good sense; from the lord's point of view it kept his administrative costs down to a minimum. The stability of the system is indicated by the fact that long-term leases for a life or for several lives were common, and that these long-term grants tended to turn into hereditary tenures.

But the steep rise in prices around 1200 created severe problems for the lord living on fixed rents. If he, rather than his tenants, were to take advantage of the market economy, then he had to switch to direct management of his manors. To abandon an age-old system was not easy and many lords encountered fierce resistance from their tenants, but gradually it was done. The most famous description of the process can be read in Jocelin of Brakelond's account of the business-like life of Abbot Samson of Bury St. Edmunds (abbot 1182–1211). The landlord took his estates into his own hands, appointed bailiffs and reeves to run them and sell the surplus on the open market. Under this new regime, the lord's expenses and profits were going to vary from year to year. This would have made it very easy for his officials to cheat him unless a close check were kept on their activities. So a detailed record of the manorial year was drawn up and then sent, together with similar returns from the other manors, to be checked by auditors who represented the central administration of a great estate. (The survival of masses of these accounts means that we know a great deal about some aspects of the thirteenth-century English rural economy.) The auditors had a policy-making as well as a fraud-detecting role. They fixed targets for each manor, the levels of production of grain and livestock which had to be reached. They took investment decisions, whether to build new barns, whether to buy fertilizers, and so on. Inspired by these concerns a whole new literature was born, treatises on agriculture and estate management, of which Walter of Henley's *Husbandry* is the most famous. All these changes presupposed the existence of widespread practical literacy: without this it would not have been possible to carry through the managerial revolution—for that is what it was—of the early thirteenth century.

The whole point of the new system was to maximize the lord's profits, and to do so in as rational a way as possible. It seems unlikely that this was an approach which was going to concern itself with the problems facing the poor, the lame ducks of the economic system, nearly all of whom were born lame. At a manorial level there are innumerable cases of resistance to a lord's demands, both passive resistance and direct, sometimes legal, action. In the towns, too, there is increasing evidence of a struggle between rich and poor. By the 1290s England was a country choked with people, a traditional economy unable to cope with the strains of population pressure, even perhaps a land on the brink of class warfare.

2. The Later Middle Ages
(1290–1485)

═══

RALPH A. GRIFFITHS

To those who lived at the time, and to many historians since, the fourteenth and fifteenth centuries seemed a dangerous, turbulent, and decadent age. England's civil and foreign wars—especially those in Scotland, France, and the Low Countries—lasted longer, extended further afield, cost more, and involved larger numbers of men than any it had fought since the Viking Age. Within the British Isles, Welshmen were distrusted by the English, despite Edward I's conquests; uprisings culminating in Owain Glyndŵr's rebellion (from 1400) seemed to justify this distrust and recall prophecies that foretold of the expulsion of the English from Wales. Celtic prejudice against Englishmen flourished with all the bitterness and resentment of which the defeated or oppressed were capable: 'The tyranny and cruelty of the English', claimed a Scot in 1442, 'are notorious throughout the world, as manifestly appears in their usurpations against the French, Scots, Welsh, Irish and neighbouring lands.' Famine, disease, and (from 1348) plague drastically reduced England's population by the early fifteenth century, perhaps by as much as a half, and this severely disrupted English society. Towards the end of the fifteenth century, French statesmen were noting with disapproval Englishmen's habit of deposing and murdering their kings and the children of kings (as happened in 1327, 1399, 1461, 1471, 1483, and 1485) with a regularity unmatched anywhere else in Western Europe. Spiritual uncertainty and the spread of heresy led the choleric Chancellor of Oxford University, Dr Thomas Gascoigne, to conclude that the English Church of his day was decayed, and its bishops and clergy failing in their duty. One popular poet, writing about 1389, thought that this seemingly decadent age was all too appropriately reflected in the extravagant and indecent fashion for padded shoulders, tightly-drawn waistbands, close-fitting hose, and long pointed shoes.

There are, of course, dangers in taking contemporaries at their own estimation, particularly if they lived at times of special tension or turmoil. It is now accepted that wars can have a creative side, in this case giving Englishmen a sharper sense of national identity; that famine and disease need not utterly prostrate a society, or economic contraction necessarily mean economic depression; that the growth of heresy and criticism of religious institutions may spur men to greater personal devotion; that, as with the evolution of Parliament, political crises have constructive features; and, finally, that literary and artistic accomplishments are rarely extinguished by civil commotion or social ferment. From the vantage point of the late twentieth century, the later Middle Ages now appear as an age of turbulence and complexity, sure enough, but also as an age of vitality, ambition, and, above all, fascination.

England at War, 1290–1390

The king and his court, with the royal family and household at its centre, were the focus and fulcrum of English government and politics. Central to both was the relationship between the king and his influential subjects: the barons or magnates first and foremost, but also country knights and esquires who often aspired to join the baronial ranks, wealthy merchants, and the bishops and talented clerks—all of whom sought patronage, position, and promotion from the Crown. A successful king was one who established a harmonious relationship with all or most of these influential subjects, for only then could political stability, effective government, and domestic peace be assured. This was no simple or easy task. The growing emphasis on the king's sovereign authority in his kingdom, reinforced by the principle (from 1216) that the Crown should pass to the eldest son of the dead monarch and by the extension of royal administration in the hands of a network of king's clerks and servants, was bound to be at the expense of the feudal, regional power of the great landowners. Yet that very principle of hereditary monarchy, while it reduced the likelihood of royal kinsmen squabbling over the Crown, made it more likely that unsuitable kings (by their youth, character, or incapacity) would sometimes wear it. Above all, the persistent warfare of the fourteenth and fifteenth centuries imposed heavier obligations on England's kings. From Edward I's reign onwards, there was no decade when Englishmen were not at war, whether overseas or in the British Isles. Every generation of Englishmen in the later Middle Ages knew the demands, strains, and consequences of war—and more intensely than their forebears.

After the civil war of Henry III's reign, a successful effort was made to reconcile England and restore domestic peace whereby the king and his subjects could re-establish a stable relationship that gave due regard to the rights and aspirations of both. The new monarch, Edward I (1272–1307), showed himself to be capable, constructive, and efficient in his government, and also determined to emphasize his position as sovereign. But his unrelenting insistence on asserting his sovereignty in all the territories of the British Isles, even those beyond the borders of his realm, began the era of perpetual war.

In Wales, he overwhelmed Gwynedd, the most vigorous and independent of the surviving native lordships, and with Llywelyn ap Gruffydd's death in 1282 the conquest of Wales was successfully completed after two hundred years of intermittent warfare. The Crown thereby expanded its territories in North and West Wales to form a principality that covered half the country; in 1301 this was conferred on the king's eldest son as the first English-born Prince of Wales. It was a notable achievement, if a costly one. Material damage had to be made good; an imaginative plan for future security included a dozen new and half-a-dozen reconstructed fortresses, most of them complemented by new walled boroughs peopled by loyal immigrants; and a permanent administration was devised for the conquered lands. This administration (announced in the statute of Rhuddlan, 1284) began as a military regime but soon established peace and stability by a judicious combination of English innovation and Welsh practice. Firmness, tempered by fairness and conciliation, was the hallmark of relations between the new governors and the Welsh population, and rebellions in 1287, 1294–5, and 1316 were not widespread or dangerous threats. Yet the costs of conquest were prodigious. Soldiers and sailors, architects, craftsmen, and labourers were recruited in every English county and beyond to serve in Wales. At least £75,000 was spent on castle-building between 1277 and 1301 alone (when a skilled mason earned less than 2s. a week), whilst the suppression of the 1294–5 revolt cost about £55,000. Fortunately, royal government in Wales proved eminently successful: by the mid-fourteenth century it was producing a profit for the royal exchequer and the Welsh gentry prospered in co-operation with an alien regime.

No sooner had Llywelyn been eliminated than Edward I turned to the lords of the Welsh march (or borderland)— mostly English magnates—to establish his sovereign rights over them and their subjects too; and he brought the Welsh Church and bishops more directly under his control. The whole enterprise of Edwardian conquest showed an imagination and determination and a grasp of strategy that went far beyond the military campaigns. But the feelings of bitterness among the conquered, who were ruled in Church and State by an alien hierarchy, could not easily be removed. If English domination were to become oppressive, if the economic benefits of stable rule dried up, or if relations between native and immigrant deteriorated, serious problems would be created for the English state, and colonial rule would be threatened.

Edward I was equally intent on exerting his superior lordship over Scotland. This was an exceptionally ambitious undertaking because Scotland, unlike Wales, had its own monarch (of the house of Canmore) and Scotsmen's sense of independence was fierce, especially in the remoter Highlands. But, as with Wales, an opportunity to assert England's overlordship had arisen in Edward's reign in 1286 on the death of King Alexander III and of his granddaughter and heiress four years later. Edward accepted the invitation of the Scottish 'guardians of the realm' to settle the succession question, and he took advantage of this 'Great Cause' (1291–2) to secure recognition of himself as 'lord superior' of Scotland. Scottish resistance and Edward's efforts to make his claim a reality began a barren period of mutual hostility between the two countries that lasted well into the sixteenth century. The Scots sought French aid (1295) and papal support, and they generated a vigorous patriotism in defence of their political independence under the leadership of William Wallace (executed 1305) and Robert Bruce (King Robert I, 1306–29). A score of English invasions in the half-century after 1296 succeeded in establishing an uneasy military and administrative presence in the Lowlands, but it was difficult to sustain in poor and hostile country and had to be financed largely from England. Nor did the English command the northern seas or subdue and control the north and west of Scotland. Thus, the English had none of the advantages—or success—that attended their ventures in Wales, and even in battle (notably at Bannockburn, 1314) their cavalry forces suffered humiliating defeat at the hands of more mobile Scotsmen. The treaty of Northampton (1328), which recognized King Robert and surrendered the English claim to overlordship, was quickly disowned by Edward III when he took personal charge of the government in 1330. Anglo-Scottish relations thereafter were a sad catalogue of invasion, border raids, unstable English occupation of southern shires, Franco-Scottish agreements that hardened into the 'Auld Alliaunce'—even the capture of King David II at Neville's Cross (1346). Scotland proved a persistent and expensive irritation after English claims and ambitions were thwarted by determined and united resistance by the Scots.

After Bannockburn, Robert I tried to forestall further English operations in Scotland by exploiting the situation in Ireland. During 1315–18 his brother, Edward Bruce, secured the support of Anglo-Irish magnates and Gaelic chiefs, and in 1316 he was declared High King of Ireland. Soon afterwards, Robert himself visited Ireland and this may have been designed to stimulate a 'pan-Celtic' movement against Edward II of England (1307–27). This Scottish intervention was a severe shock to the English government and revealed the weakness of its regime in Dublin. No English king visited Ireland between 1210 and 1394—not even Edward I, conqueror of the Welsh and 'hammer of the Scots'. Instead, Edward I ruthlessly stripped the country of its resources of men, money, and supplies, especially for his wars and castle-building in Wales and Scotland. Harsh exploitation and absentee rule led in time to administrative abuse and the decay of order, of which the Anglo-Irish magnates and Gaelic chiefs took full advantage. The king's officials presided over an increasingly feeble and neglected administration, whilst a Gaelic political and cultural revival had taken root in the thirteenth century. This contributed to the success of Edward Bruce, during whose ascendancy Ireland, said a contemporary, 'became one trembling wave of commotion'. The English lordship never recovered and henceforward was unable to impose its authority throughout the island. Instead of being a financial resource, Ireland became a financial liability, with a revenue after 1318 that was a third of what it had been under Edward I and therefore quite inadequate to sustain English rule. Periodic expeditions led by minor figures could do little to revive the king's authority and the area under direct rule consequently contracted to the 'pale' around Dublin. It was a confession of failure when the government resorted to racial and cultural separation, even persecution, by a series of enactments culminating in the statute of Kilkenny (1366). The 'lord of

Ireland' had a perfunctory lordship in the later Middle Ages that was costly, lawless, hostile to English rule, and open to exploitation by the Scots, the French, and even by Welsh rebels.

The recognition of overlordship which English monarchs demanded of the Welsh, Scots, and Irish was denied to the French king in Gascony, where these same English kings, as dukes of Aquitaine, had been feudal vassals of the Crown of France since 1204. Gascony lay at the heart of Anglo-French relations both before and during the so-called Hundred Years War (1337–1453): it replaced Normandy and Anjou as the main bone of contention. At Edward I's accession, this prosperous, wine-producing province was England's only remaining French territory, and the political link with England was reinforced by a flourishing export trade in non-sweet wine which was complemented by the transport of English cloth and corn by sea to Bordeaux and Bayonne: in 1306–7 the duchy's revenue was about £17,000 and well worth fighting for. Friction with the French king over Gascony's frontier and the rights of Gascons was gradually subsumed in the larger issues of nationhood and sovereignty posed by an assertive, self-conscious French state bent on tightening its control over its provinces and vassals (including the English duke of Aquitaine). For their part, Edward I and his successors were reluctant to see French royal rights emphasized or given any practical meaning in Gascony. The result was a series of incidents, peace conferences, 'brush-fire' wars in which French armies penetrated Gascony and the duchy was periodically confiscated, and English expeditions— even a visit by Edward I himself (1286–9).

Relations between England and France might have continued to fester in this fashion had it not been for two other factors. The English government resented the Franco-Scottish alliance (from 1295) and was angered by the refuge offered by the French (1334) to the Scottish King David II after Edward III had invaded Scotland. Even more contentious were the consequences of the approaching extinction of the senior male line of the French royal house of Capet. The deaths, in rapid succession, of four French kings between 1314 and 1328, requiring the swearing of homage for Gascony on each occasion, were irritating enough, but the demise of the last Capet in 1328 raised the question of the succession to the French throne itself. At that point, the new English king, Edward III (1327–77), was in no position to stake his own claim through his French mother, Isabella, but in 1337, when the Gascon situation had deteriorated further, he did so. His action may have been primarily tactical, to embarrass the new Valois monarch, Philip VI, though for an English king to become king of France would have the undeniable merit of resolving at a stroke the difficult Gascon issue: the political stability and economic prosperity of Gascony would be assured. Thus, when a French fleet was sighted off the Norman coast *en route* (so the English believed) for Scotland in 1337, war began—and would last for more than a century.

England's war aims were neither constant nor consistently pursued. Especially in the fourteenth century, its war diplomacy was primarily dictated by a series of immediate problems, notably, of how to maintain independent rule in Gascony and how to deter Scottish attacks across the northern border in support of the French. Even after Edward III claimed the French Crown in 1337, he was prepared to ransom John II, the French king captured at the battle of Poitiers (1356), and to abandon his claim in the treaty of Brétigny (1360) in return for practical concessions. Nevertheless, dynastic ties, commercial and strategic considerations, even differing attitudes to the Papacy, which was installed at Avignon from 1308 to 1378, combined to extend the Anglo-French conflict to the Low Countries, to Castile and Portugal, as well as to Scotland, Ireland, and even Wales. To begin with, the wars (for this was a disjointed series of conflicts rather than one war) were fought by sieges in northern France in 1338–40; then there was more intensive campaigning by pincer movements through the French provinces of Brittany, Gascony, and Normandy in 1341–7 (resulting in the English victory at Crécy and the capture of Calais).

This was followed by bold marches or *chevauchées* by Edward III's eldest son, Edward the Black Prince, from Gascony in 1355–6 (culminating in the great victory at Poitiers) and by the king himself in 1359 to Rheims, the traditional coronation seat of French kings. The renewal of war in Castile (1367) inaugurated a period of more modest and fitful campaigning in Portugal, Flanders, and France itself, with both sides gradually exhausting themselves.

The advantage in the war lay initially with England, the more united and better organized of the two kingdoms. Its prosperity, based especially on wool production, and its experience of warfare in Wales and Scotland, were invaluable foundations for larger-scale operations on mainland Europe. The existence of highly independent French provinces dictated English strategy. Edward III's campaigns in the Low Countries in 1338–40 relied on the support of the cloth-manufacturing cities of Flanders which, though subject to the French king, had vital commercial links with England. In the 1340s a succession dispute in Brittany enabled English forces to intervene there and even to garrison certain castles; while Gascony, though far to the south, afforded direct access to central France.

The wars within the British Isles gave the English government a unique opportunity to develop novel methods of raising substantial forces. Supplementing and gradually replacing the traditional feudal array, the newer paid, contracted armies, recruited by indentured captains, were smaller, better disciplined, and more dependable and flexible than the loosely organized and ponderous French forces. English men-at-arms and archers, proficient in the use of the longbow and employing defensive tactics in battle, had a decisive advantage which brought resounding victories against all the odds in the early decades of the war (most notably at Crécy and Poitiers). The war at sea was a more minor affair, with naval tactics showing little novelty or imagination. It was usually beyond the capability of fourteenth-century commanders to stage a naval engagement and the battle of Sluys (which the English won in 1340) was incidental to Edward III's expedition to Flanders. The English never kept a fleet permanently in being, but the Valois, learning the expertise of their Castilian allies, later constructed dockyards at Rouen which in time gave them an edge at sea (witness their victory off La Rochelle in 1372).

English investment in the French war was immense and unprecedented. Expeditions were organized with impressive regularity and were occasionally very large (over 10,000 men in 1346–7, for instance). The financial outlay was prodigious and tolerated so long as the war was successful; but as the margin of England's military advantage narrowed after 1369, so the government resorted to newer and more desperate expedients, including poll taxes. Shipping for defence and expeditions could not be supplied solely by the traditional obligation of the southern Cinque Ports, and hundreds of merchant vessels (735 for the siege of Calais in 1347, for example) were impressed and withdrawn from normal commercial operations. Coastal defence against French and Castilian raiders, who grew bolder after 1369, was organized by the maritime shires of the south and east, supported by others inland—but even this could not prevent the sacking of Winchelsea (1360), Rye (1377), and other ports. The costs of war were indeed high. It is true that conquered French estates were enjoyed by many a fortunate soldier, and ransoms were profitable during the victorious years (King John II's ransom alone was fixed at £500,000). But the lives and occupations of thousands of Englishmen, Welshmen, and Irishmen were disrupted by war service; supplies of food, materials, and equipment were diverted to operations that were entirely destructive; and the wool and wine trades were severely hampered. What is remarkable is that England was able to engage in these enterprises overseas for decades without serious political or social strains at home, and at the same time to defend the Scottish border, keep the Welsh calm, and avoid Irish uprisings. This achievement owed much to the inspiration, example, and leadership of Edward III and the Black Prince, both of whom embodied the chivalric virtues vaunted by the nobility and admired by society at large. To Jean Froissart, the Hainaulter who knew them both and kept a record of the most inspiring chivalric deeds of his age, the king was 'gallant and noble [whose] like had not been seen since the days of King Arthur'. His son appeared as 'this most gallant man and chivalrous prince' who, at his death in 1376, a year before Edward III himself died, 'was deeply mourned for his noble qualities'. King Edward presided over a regime in England that was less harsh than Edward I's and far more capable than Edward II's.

These wars were a catalyst of social change, constitutional development, and political conflict in England which would otherwise have occurred more slowly. Moreover, along with the rest of Europe, England in the fourteenth century experienced population and economic fluctuations that increased tension and uncertainty. The result was a series of crises which underlined how delicately balanced was the relationship between the king and his subjects (especially his magnates, who regarded themselves as representing the entire 'community of the realm') and how crucial to a personal monarchy was the king himself. Able and determined—even far-sighted—Edward I and his advisers may have been, but the king's obstinate and autocratic nature seriously strained relations with his influential subjects. Between 1290 and 1297, the propertied classes, the merchants, and especially the clergy were subjected to extraordinarily heavy and novel demands for taxes (four times as frequently as in the first half of Edward's reign) for the king's enterprises in France and the British Isles. There was resistance and a property tax of 1297 produced only a fraction (£35,000) of what had been anticipated. Further, armies had been summoned by the king for prolonged service outside the realm. Edward's attempts to silence resistance shocked the clergy and embittered the merchants. The leading magnates, including Welsh marcher lords who resented Edward's invasion of their cherished franchises, reacted by resuming their time-honoured role as self-appointed spokesmen of the realm, and they presented grievances to the king in 1297 and again in 1300. They deployed Magna Carta as their banner against taxation without the payers' consent, and against oppressive and unprecedented exactions. Yet, when Edward died in the arms of his attendants at Burgh-by-Sands on 7 July 1307, just as he was about to cross the Solway Firth on his sixth expedition to Scotland, the problems of wartime remained. He bequeathed to his son and successor, Edward II (1307–27), an expensive war in the north that was nowhere near a victorious conclusion, and political unrest in England compounded by a dwindling of trust between monarch and subject. These two preoccupations—political stability and war—dominated public affairs during the following 200 years and had a profound effect on the kingdom's social and political cohesion and on its economic prosperity. The new king would need exceptional tact if a further crisis of authority were to be avoided.

Tact was not Edward II's outstanding quality. Starved of affection during childhood, ignored by his father in adolescence, and confronted by unsolved problems at his accession, Edward II sought advice, friendship, even affection, from ambitious favourites such as Peter Gavaston and Hugh Despenser who were unworthy of the king's trust and whose influence was resented by many magnates. These facts, together with the determination of the magnates (led by Thomas, earl of Lancaster) to extract from Edward concessions and reforms which Edward I had been unwilling to confirm, turned the formidable difficulties of ruling a kingdom that was facing setbacks in Scotland, Ireland, Wales, and France into a struggle for political reform and personal advancement. An extended and more specific coronation oath (1308) bound the new king more firmly to observe English law and custom, and ordinances drawn up by the magnates in 1311 sought to limit the king's freedom of action; these ordinances were announced in Parliament in order to gain wide support and approval. Edward II had all the stubbornness of his father (though without his ability) and Gavaston's murder (1312) converted this quality into an unshakeable resolve not to be dominated by his friend's murderers.

Meanwhile, the burdens of war and defence on the king's subjects were scarcely less heavy than they had been during Edward I's conquests, and this at a time of severe social distress and poverty caused by a succession of disastrous harvests and livestock diseases during 1315–22. Civil war (1321–2) and the king's deposition (1326–7) were the fateful outcome of the failure of king and governed to co-operate to mutual benefit. Edward denounced the ordinances in 1322, again in a Parliament (at York), and after the defeat of his opponents at Boroughbridge in 1322, he executed Lancaster. By 1326, Edward's deposition in favour of his namesake son and heir seemed the only alternative to a mean, oppressive, and unsuccessful regime that engendered civil strife. This awesome step, engineered with Queen Isabella's connivance, the acquiescence of Prince Edward, and with substantial magnate and other support, demonstrated in a Parliament, was unprecedented: since the Norman Conquest, no English king had been deposed from his throne. In 1327, therefore, every effort was made to conceal the unconcealable and justify the unjustifiable. Browbeaten, tearful, and half-fainting, the wretched king was forced to assent to his own abdication, and a meeting of Parliament was used to spread the responsibility as widely as possible. Although the accession of Edward's son ensured that the hereditary principle remained intact, the inviolability of anointed kingship had been breached.

Although only fifteen in 1327, Edward III was soon a parent and proved far more capable than his father and more sensitive than he to the attitudes and aspirations of his magnates— indeed, he shared them, particularly in warfare and in accepting the chivalric obligations of an aristocratic society. At the same time, the new king's grandiose and popular plans in France raised issues similar to those posed by Edward I's enterprises in the British Isles and Gascony. Should these plans ultimately prove unsuccessful, the implications for England might well be similar to those that had surfaced in Edward II's reign. The outbreak of prolonged war in 1337 meant increased taxation at a level even higher than that of Edward I's last years, and Edward III showed the same ruthlessness towards merchants, bankers, and landowners as Edward I had done. Moreover, the absences of the king on campaign, in the thick of the fighting which he and his magnates relished, posed serious questions for a sophisticated administration normally under the personal direction of the king. Edward's ordinances (issued at Walton-on-Thames, 1338) for the government of England from abroad caused friction between the king and his advisers in northern France on the one hand, and those councillors remaining in England on the other. Some even feared that, if the war were successful, England might take second place in King Edward's mind to his realm of France. Thus, in 1339–43 another crisis arose in which magnates, merchants, and the Commons in Parliament (now the forum in which royal demands for taxation were made) protested to the king. Edward was induced to act more circumspectly and considerately towards his magnates, clergy, and subjects generally. The eventual reconciliation, and the re-establishment of the trust in the king that had proved so elusive since the 1290s, was possible because Edward III was a sensible and pragmatic monarch, with a self-confidence that did not extend to arrogance. He appointed ministers acceptable to his magnates, he pandered to the self-importance of Parliament, and he developed a remarkable *rapport* with his subjects which sustained his rule in England and his ambitions in France for a quarter of a century. Further crisis was avoided, despite England's involvement in its most major war yet.

There was an enormous contrast with the situation in the 1370s and 1380s. For the generation of Englishmen alive then, the frustrations of the resumed war in France (from 1369) and of debilitating skirmishes in Ireland and on the Scottish border were unsettling; and renewed taxation, after a decade when England had enjoyed the profits of war and a respite from taxes, was resented. Raids on south-coast ports were frequent, uncertain naval control of the Channel imperilled trade and upset the merchants, and expensive *chevauchées* in France were occasionally spectacular but rarely profitable. Yet the abrupt reversal of English policy in 1375, involving a humiliating truce with France and payments to the mistrusted pope, only served to affront and exasperate Englishmen. Moreover, after the death (1369) of Queen Philippa, a paragon among queens, Edward III lapsed gently into a senility that sapped his strength and impaired his judgement. The Black Prince, too, began to suffer from the effects of his wartime exertions; in fact, he predeceased his father in June 1376. Yet the financial, man-power, and other burdens on England's population were not eased. Questions were raised, especially by the Commons in Parliament, about the honesty as well as the competence of the king's advisers and officials. Strengthened by a rising tide of anti-clericalism in an age when the reputation of the Papacy and the Church was severely tarnished, the outcry had swept Edward III's clerical ministers from power in 1371 and others were accused of corruption, even treason. Another political crisis had arisen. In the 'Good Parliament' of 1376, the longest and most dramatic assembly yet held, the allegedly corrupt and incapable ministers—even the old king's influential mistress, Alice Perrers—were accused by the Commons and tried before the Lords in a novel and highly effective procedure (impeachment) which henceforward enabled persons in high places to be held publicly to account for their public actions.

The crisis entered a new phase when King Edward himself died in June 1377. He was succeeded by the Black Prince's only surviving son and heir, Richard II (1377–99), who was ten years of age. England was faced with the prospect of only the second royal minority since 1066 and the first since 1216. On the latter occasion there had followed a period of political turbulence centring on the young Henry III; a similar situation developed after 1377 and played its part in precipitating the Peasants' Revolt (1381) in eastern and south-eastern England. A series of poll taxes was imposed during 1377–80 to finance the war. These taxes were at a rate higher than was usual and the tax of

1379 was popularly known as 'the evil subsidy'. They sparked off violence in East Anglia against the tax-collectors and the justices who tried to force compliance on the population. But what turned these irritations into widespread rebellion was the prolonged dislocation of unsuccessful war, the impact of recurrent plagues, and the anticlerical temper of the times. Hopes of remedy placed by the rebels in the young King Richard proved to be vain, though he showed considerable courage in facing the rebels in London during the summer of 1381.

Richard was still only fourteen, and the aristocratic rivalries in the ruling circle continued, not least among the king's uncles. This and the lack of further military success in France damaged the reputation of the council that governed England in Richard's name and even affected the king's own standing in the eyes of his subjects. Richard, too, was proving a self-willed monarch whose sense of insecurity led him to depend on unworthy favourites reminiscent of Edward II's confidants. As he grew older, he naturally wanted to expand his entourage and his household beyond what had been appropriate for a child. Among his friends and associates were some who were new to the ranks of the aristocracy, and all were generously patronized by the king at the expense of those (including his uncle Gloucester) who did not attract Richard's favour. In 1386 Parliament and a number of magnates attacked Richard's closest associates and even threatened the king himself. With all the stubbornness of the Plantagenets, Richard refused to yield. This led to further indictments or appeals of his advisers by five leading 'appellant' lords (the duke of Gloucester, and the earls of Warwick, Arundel, Nottingham, and Derby, the king's cousin), and a skirmish took place at Radcot Bridge in December 1387 when the king's closest friend, the earl of Oxford, was routed. At the momentous 'Merciless Parliament' (1388), the king was forced to submit to aristocratic correction which, if it had been sustained, would have significantly altered the character of the English monarchy. Once again, the pressures of war, the tensions of personal rule, and the ambitions of England's magnates had produced a most serious political and constitutional crisis. The institution of hereditary monarchy emerged largely unscathed after a century and more of such crises, but criticism of the king's advisers had reached a new level of effectiveness and broader sections of opinion had exerted a significant influence on events. These were the political and personal dimensions of more deep-seated changes that were transforming England's social and economic life in the later Middle Ages.

Wealth, Population, and Social Change

England's wealth in the later Middle Ages was its land, the exploitation of which engaged most Englishmen: growing corn, producing dairy goods, and tending livestock. England's most important industry, textiles, was indirectly based on the land, producing the finest wool in Europe from often very large sheep flocks: St. Peter's Abbey, Gloucester, owned over 10,000 sheep by 1300, when the total number in England is thought to have been in the region of fifteen to eighteen millions. The wealthiest regions were the lowlands and gently rolling hill-country of the midland and southern shires, with extensions into the borderland and southern littoral of Wales. Other industries were less significant in creating wealth and employing labour, but Cornish tin-mining was internationally famous and the tin was exported to the Continent. Lead, iron, and coal mining was quite modest, though the coastal traffic in coal from the Tyne Valley and the neighbourhood of Swansea reflected its growing domestic and industrial use. As for financial and commercial services, the economy gained little from what became, in modern times, one of the nation's prime sources of wealth. Few English merchants—the de la Poles of Hull were an exception—could compete with the international bankers of Italy, with their branches in London, despite the fact that Edward I and Edward III were slow to honour their war debts to these Italian companies. England's mercantile marine was generally outclassed, except in coastal waters, by foreign shipping; but the Gascon wine-run and woollen shipments to the Low Countries did fall increasingly into the hands of English merchants and into the holds of English vessels. The thousand and more markets and fairs dotted about the English and Welsh countryside—more numerous by 1350 than in the past—served mainly their local community within a radius of a score or so miles. Most of these small towns and villages—Monmouth, Worcester, and Stratford among them—were integrated with their rural hinterland, whose well-to-do inhabitants frequently played a part in town life, joining the guilds, buying or renting town residences, and filling urban offices. A small number of towns, including some ports, were larger and had broader commercial horizons: Shrewsbury's traders travelled regularly to London by the fifteenth century, and merchants from the capital and Calais (after 1347) visited the Welsh borderland in search of fine wool. Bristol, with its vital link with Bordeaux, was rapidly becoming the entrepôt of late medieval Severnside; whilst York, Coventry, and especially London were centres of international trade.

From this wealth sprang the prosperity of individuals, institutions, and the Crown. The greatest landowners were the lay magnates (small in number, like 'skyscrapers on a plain'), bishops, monasteries, and other religious institutions. In 1300 these still benefited handsomely from a market boom created by the expanding population of the previous century. Prices were buoyant and landed incomes substantial: after the earl of Gloucester died at Bannockburn (1314), his estates were estimated to be worth just over £6,000 a year, whilst those of Christ Church Priory, Canterbury, produced in 1331 a gross annual income of more than £2,540. Landowners therefore exploited their estates directly and took a personal interest in their efficient management. They insisted on their rights as far as possible, squeezing higher rents out of tenants and carefully recording in manor courts the obligations attached to holdings. Such landed wealth was the foundation of the political, administrative, and social influence of the aristocracy, many of whom had estates in several counties as well as Wales and Ireland: Humphrey, earl of Hereford and Essex, for instance, inherited property in Essex, Middlesex, Huntingdonshire, Hertfordshire, and Buckinghamshire, and also in Brecon, Hay, Huntington, and Caldicot in the Welsh march. Land was equally the basis of the gentry's fortunes, albeit on a more local, shire level; whilst it gave ecclesiastical landowners an earthly authority that complemented their hold on men's minds and souls. This wealth could support pretensions and ambitions on a more national stage, as in the case of Thomas, earl of Lancaster, the richest earl in the England of his day.

The peasantry in 1300 were living in a world where land was scarce and opportunities for economic advancement were limited by the tight controls of the landowners. Prices were high— the price of wheat after 1270 was consistently higher than it had been earlier in the century—and there was little cash to spare after food, clothing, and equipment had been bought. Wages in an over-stocked labour market were low and reduced the purchasing power of skilled and unskilled alike: a carpenter earned 3*d.* a day (without food) and a labourer 1*d.* or 1½*d.* Grumbles, complaints, and spasms of violence were directed at landowners and their officials, and rent strikes and refusals to perform customary labour services were not uncommon.

The merchants of 1300, most notably the exporters of wool and importers of wine, thrived in an expanding market from the Baltic to Spain, Portugal, and, especially after the opening of the sea-route from the Mediterranean, to northern Italy. During 1304–11 wool exports averaged annually 39,500 sacks (each containing at least 250 fleeces) and only 30–40 per cent of these cargoes was shipped by foreigners. The rising antipathy towards alien merchants in English trade reflects the self-confidence and assertiveness of native (or denizen) merchants. Edward I legislated (1280s) in their interest, notably to facilitate the recovery of debts at law, which was essential to the expansion of trade. But when war came, merchants were among the

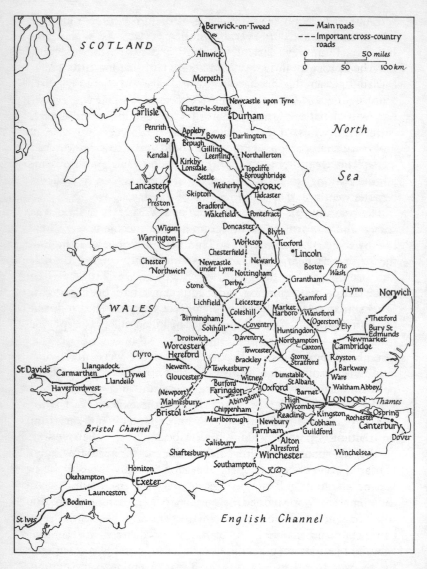

MAIN ROADS IN MEDIEVAL ENGLAND AND WALES

first to resist heavy taxation, especially the *maltolt* (or 'evil tax') of 1294, and the impressment of their ships.

The king was the largest landowner of all, even before Edward I acquired a principality in Wales and the estates of the house of Lancaster merged with the Crown's in 1399. The growth of national taxation under Edward I and his successors enabled the Crown to tap the wealth of private landowners and merchants, too. Not even the peasantry escaped, as was well appreciated by those who sang the popular lament, 'Song of the Husbandman', in Edward I's reign. Then, in 1327, all who had goods worth at least 10s. a year were required to pay 1s. 8d. in tax, and doubtless the less well-off had the burden passed on to them indirectly. The preoccupation with war made the king heavily dependent on the wealth and forbearance of his subjects. If that wealth ceased to grow, or if the prosperity of individuals and institutions were punctured, then the king's extraordinary commitments might eventually be beyond his means and his subjects' tolerance wear dangerously thin.

By the mid-fourteenth century the prosperous period of 'high farming' was almost over. Prices were falling, making cultivation for a market less profitable. Wages were rising, more so for agricultural labourers than for craftsmen, and there was no advantage in employing women, who were paid the same as men—indeed, in bear-baiting they were paid more! The principal reason why large-scale farming was losing some of its attraction was that the population boom came to an end and went, full throttle, into reverse. As the pool of available labour shrank, wages rose; as the population declined so did the demand for food and supplies, and prices followed suit.

England's population reached its peak, perhaps over four millions, about the end of the thirteenth century. At that time, there was insufficient cultivable land to ensure that all peasant families had an adequate livelihood. A high population coupled with low living standards inevitably meant poverty, famine, and disease, and a mortality that crept upwards and brought the demographic boom to a halt. The plight of those living at or below the poverty-line was made worse by a series of natural disasters related to over-exploitation of the land and exceptionally bad weather in the opening decades of the fourteenth century. Poor harvests were calamitous for a society without adequate storage facilities: there was less to eat and no cash to buy what now cost much more. The harvests of the years 1315, 1316, 1320, and 1321 were exceptionally bad; cattle and sheep murrains were especially prevalent in 1319 and 1321, and on the estates of Ramsey Abbey (Cambs.) recovery took twenty years; and in 1324–6 parts of England had severe floods which drowned thousands of sheep in Kent. Famine and disease spread, and on Halesowen Manor (Worcs.) 15 per cent of males died in 1315–17. Agricultural dislocation was widespread, grain prices soared (from 5s. 7¼d. to 26s. 8d. per quarter in Halesowen during 1315–16), and wool exports collapsed. However, it was a temporary calamity and England gradually recovered during the 1320s; but the vulnerability of the poor in particular had been starkly demonstrated.

Longer lasting and more profound were the consequences of plague. The first attack, known since the late sixteenth century as the Black Death but to contemporaries as 'the great mortality', occurred in southern England in 1348; by the end of 1349 it had spread north to central Scotland. Geoffrey le Baker, a contemporary Oxfordshire cleric, described its progress from the ports, where it arrived in rat-infested ships, and men's helplessness in diagnosing its cause and dealing with its effects.

And at first it carried off almost all the inhabitants of the seaports in Dorset, and then those living inland and from there it raged so dreadfully through Devon and Somerset as far as Bristol and then men of Gloucester refused those of Bristol entrance to their country, everyone thinking that the breath of those who lived amongst people who died of plague was infectious. But at last it attacked Gloucester, yea and Oxford and London, and finally the whole of England so violently that scarcely one in ten of either sex was left alive. As the graveyards did not suffice, fields were chosen for the burial of the dead . . . A countless number of common people and a host of monks and nuns and clerics as well, known to God alone, passed away. It was the young and strong that the plague chiefly attacked ... This great pestilence, which began at Bristol on [15 August] and in London about [29 September], raged for a whole year in England so terribly that it cleared many country villages entirely of every human being.

While this great calamity was devastating England, the Scots rejoicing thought that they would obtain all they wished against the English ... But sorrow following on the heels of joy, the sword of the anger of God departing from the English drove the Scots to frenzy ... In the following year it ravaged the Welsh as well as the English; and at last, setting sail, so to speak, for Ireland, it laid low the English living there in great numbers, but scarcely touched at all the pure Irish who lived amongst the mountains and on higher ground, until the year of Christ 1357, when it unexpectedly and terribly destroyed them also everywhere.

At a stroke, the Black Death reduced England's population by about a third. By 1350, Newcastle upon Tyne was in desperate financial straits 'on account of the deadly pestilence as by various other adversities in these times of war', and Carlisle was 'wasted and more than usually depressed as well by the mortal pestilence lately prevalent in those parts as by frequent attacks' (by the Scots). Seaford (Sussex) was reported even in 1356 as 'so desolated by plague and the chances of war that men living there are so few and poor that they cannot pay their taxes or defend the town'. Tusmore (Oxon.) was another victim of the plague: by 1358 permission was given to turn its fields into a park because every villein was dead and the village no longer had any taxpayers. Nevertheless, the Black Death's effects were not immediately or permanently catastrophic. The behaviour of a Welshman living in Ruthin was not uncommon: he 'left his land during the pestilence on account of poverty', but by 1354 he had returned 'and was admitted by the lord's favour to hold the same land by the service due from the same'. In any case, in a well-populated country, dead tenants could be replaced and landowners' incomes over the next twenty years were cut by no more than 10 per cent. It was the recurrence of plague over the following century—particularly the attacks of 1360–2, 1369, and 1375—which had lasting effects, even if these outbreaks were more local and urban. The population steadily declined to about $2\frac{1}{2}$ millions—or even less—by the mid-fifteenth century.

For those who survived an ugly death, life may not have been as wretched in the late fourteenth and fifteenth centuries as it undoubtedly was before. For many peasants, this became an age of opportunity, ambition, and affluence: Chaucer was able to portray his pilgrims in the *Canterbury Tales* with good-humoured optimism, not in an atmosphere of gloom and despondency. The peasant in a smaller labour market was often able to shake off the disabilities of centuries, force rents down, and insist on a better wage for his hire; and with the collapse in prices, his standard of living rose. The more successful and ambitious peasants leased new property, invested spare cash by lending to their fellows and, especially in the south and east, built substantial stone houses for the first time in peasant history.

Landowners, on the other hand, were facing severe difficulties. Market production in wheat, wool, and other commodities was less profitable, the cultivated area of England contracted, and agricultural investment was curtailed. Wages and other costs climbed and it seemed advisable to abandon 'high farming' techniques in favour of leasing plots to enterprising peasants. Entire communities were deserted—the 'lost villages' of England—and many of these were abandoned as a result of the twin afflictions of demographic crisis and prolonged war: among the English regions with the highest number of 'lost' villages' are Northumberland, close to the Scottish border, and the Isle of Wight, the goal of enemy marauders. Only in the last decades of the fifteenth century—from the 1460s in East Anglia—did England's population begin to rise at all significantly, and it is likely that the level of 1300 was not reached again until the seventeenth century.

England's economy had contracted markedly in the late fourteenth century, but it was not universally depressed. After men came to terms with the psychological shock of the plague visitations, society adjusted remarkably well, though not without turmoil. Landowners had the most painful adjustment to make and they reacted in several ways, not all of which were calculated to preserve domestic peace. Some, including the more conservatively-minded ecclesiastical landlords such as the abbot of St. Albans, resorted to high-handed measures, even to oppression and extortion, to preserve their hold on their remaining tenants. Some exploited their estates ruthlessly in order to conserve their incomes, and the harsh attitudes of magnate families such as the Mortimers, with extensive estates in Wales, may have helped cause the Glyndŵr rebellion (1400). Others, such as the dukes of Buckingham later in the fifteenth century, adopted more efficient methods of management to improve the profitability of their estates. Yet others saw the enclosure of fields and commons for pasture and cultivation as less costly and an alternative means of buttressing unsteady rent-rolls; enclosure gathered speed especially in the north and west in the later fifteenth century. Large and small, the landowners as a group acted 'to curb the malice of servants, who were idle, and not willing to serve after the pestilence, without excessive wages'. Edward III's ordinance (1349) to restore pre-plague wage levels and discourage mobility among an emancipated labour force was quickly turned into a parliamentary statute (1351). Moreover, the well-placed magnate or gentleman had supplementary sources of wealth available to him: royal patronage in the form of grants of land, money, and office (as the Beaufort relatives of King Henry VI well knew); family inheritance, which enabled Richard, duke of York (d. 1460) to become the richest magnate of his age; and fortunate marriage with a well-endowed heiress or a wealthy widow. Others prospered in the king's service, not least in war. Henry V's spectacular victories enabled the capture of ransomable prisoners and the acquisition of estates in northern France, and as late as

1448 the duke of Buckingham was expecting more than £530 a year from the French county of Perche. Some invested the profits of service and war in the mid-fifteenth century in the grandest manner, building imposing and elegant castles: witness Sir John Fastolf's at Caister (Norfolk), or the Herberts' huge fortress-palace at Raglan (Gwent), or Sir Ralph Botiller's castle at Sudeley, Gloucestershire. Such means and resources as these facilitated the emergence of aristocratic lines that were every whit as powerful as those of earlier centuries and often with entrenched regional positions like those of the Nevilles and Percies in the north and the Staffords and Mortimers in the west.

Similar adjustments were taking place in English towns and trade. Wool-growing remained the main pastoral occupation, but the pattern of its industry was transformed during the fourteenth century. Partly as a result of the war and its disruption of Flemish industry, and partly as a result of changes in English taste and demand, cloth manufacture absorbed growing quantities of wool previously exported; a number of the wool ports, such as Boston and Lynn in eastern England, began to decline. Leading cloth-manufacturing centres such as Stamford and Lincoln were overtaken by a host of newer ones sited in villages and towns near fast-flowing streams and rivers that ran the fulling mills. York found itself upstaged by Leeds, Halifax, and Bradford; further south, East Anglia, the west country, and even Wales developed a flourishing cloth industry, with Bristol as the main outlet in the west. London was in a class of its own: the only medieval English town with a population probably in excess of 50,000 in the late fourteenth century. It was an entrepôt for the kingdom, a terminal of the Baltic, North Sea, and Mediterranean trades; it attracted immigrants from the home counties and East Anglia, and especially from the East Midlands; and its suburbs were creeping up-river towards Westminster. No less than in the countryside, these changes unsettled life in a number of towns, whose burgess oligarchies strove to maintain their control in a changing world. The landowners of England thus strove to counter the economic crisis, but it was often at the price of straining relations with an increasingly assertive peasantry and established urban communities.

The cumulative effect of economic, social, political, and military strains in fourteenth-century England is seen most graphically in the Peasants' Revolt (1381). It was exceptional in its intensity, length, and broad appeal, but not in its fundamental character which was revealed in other conspiracies and insurrections in the years that followed. Widespread violence was sparked off in 1381 by yet another poll tax, this one at 1s. a head, three times the rate of 1377 and 1379. People responded with evasion, violence towards the collectors and the justices who investigated and, ultimately, in June 1381, with rebellion. Agricultural workers from eastern and south-eastern England were joined by townsmen and Londoners; the grain- and wool-growing countryside of East Anglia had felt the full impact of the contraction and dislocation of the economy and the social contradictions of an increasingly outmoded feudal society. Moreover, the rebels were disillusioned by the political mismanagement of the 1370s and the recent dismal record in France, and they feared enemy raids on the coast. Although heretics played no major role in the rebellion, radical criticism of the doctrines and organization of the English Church predisposed many to denounce an establishment that seemed to be failing in its duty.

Pressure on the government and an appeal to the new king ('With King Richard and the true-hearted commons' was the rebels' watch-word) held out the best hope for remedy of grievances, and the populace of London offered a pool of potential sympathizers. The rebels accordingly converged on London from Essex and Kent (where Wat Tyler and a clerical demagogue, John Ball, emerged as leaders). They threw prisons open, sacked the homes of the king's ministers, ransacked the Tower, and tried to frighten Richard II into making far-reaching concessions which, if implemented, would have broken the remain-

ing bonds of serfdom and revolutionized landholding in Church
and State. But the rebellion was poorly planned and organized
and more in the nature of a spontaneous outburst of frustra-
tion. By 15 June the rebels had dispersed to their homes.

Still at War, *1390–1490*

In 1389, when Richard II was twenty-two years old, he declared: 'I am of full age to govern my house, and my household,
and also my realm. For it seems unjust to me that the condition
which I am now in should be worse than the condition of the
least of my kingdom.' The events of 1386–8, when the appellant
lords sought to dictate the choice of the king's friends and
ministers and to regulate his political actions, had poisoned
relations between the unforgiving king and his critics. Among
these were some of the most powerful magnates in the realm,
with estates in central and southern England that together
rivalled in size the remoter franchises of the Crown in Wales,
Cheshire, and Cornwall. After 1389, however, Richard cautiously asserted himself as king of England, and with intelli-
gence and courage he tried to deal with the consequences of his
predecessors' ambitions and policies during the previous century. In a period of comparative political calm, Richard carefully constructed a party of loyalists, based on his household and
the distant franchises, particularly Cheshire and North Wales.
The earl of Arundel's forfeited lordships gave him an enhanced
royal power in the Welsh march, where aristocratic lordships
were at their most independent. The large and expensive expedition to Ireland in 1394–5, the first by an English king since
1210, was successful in revitalizing English rule and bringing
Gaelic and Anglo-Irish lords to heel by a skilful mixture of
firmness and conciliation; Richard may even have had the final
and long-delayed conquest of the island in mind. This venture
certainly strengthened his power in yet another royal lordship
and demonstrated what his household organization and resources could achieve, albeit temporarily. Towards Scotland,

following the English defeat at Otterburn (1388), Richard took the more traditional paths of encouraging dissident Scottish magnates and planning military campaigns; but in the 1390s he came to appreciate the benefits of peace. A treaty with France in 1396 and Richard's marriage to Isabella of Valois halted an even more debilitating war; if the cessation of hostilities had run its intended course (to 1426), it would have provided the longest period of peace in the entire Hundred Years War. At home, the king was able to concentrate on restoring royal government which had been so seriously damaged by the personal and political weaknesses of the 1370s and 1380s. To this end, ceremony and visual symbolism were creatively used as royal propaganda.

Richard was imaginative, shrewd, and masterful. Other of his attributes were less desirable in a king. His upbringing and adolescent experiences bred an insecurity that led to over-confidence, a lack of proportion, and arbitrariness. Wilfully extravagant towards his friends, he could be capricious, secretive, and harsh towards his enemies, and in 1397–8 he exiled the earl of Warwick, executed Arundel, murdered Gloucester, and then exiled Derby and Nottingham too. Ruthlessly deploying the monarch's personal powers ('He threw down whomsoever violated the Royal Prerogative' was part of the inscription he composed for his own tomb), Richard's last two years have been justly termed tyrannous. The pope was induced to threaten excommunication against any who 'attempts anything prejudicial against the right of our Crown, our regality or our liberty, or maliciously defames our person', while Richard's treaty with France promised French aid against his own subjects should the need arise. His second visit to Ireland in May 1399 presented Henry Bolingbroke, earl of Derby and now duke of Hereford and Lancaster, with the opportunity to return to England, retrieve his position, and recover the duchy of Lancaster estates of his father that had recently been seized by Richard. The king's methods had outrun English law and custom—and the tolerance of his greater subjects. But his deposition later in the year (29 September) ended the most coherent attempt yet to lift the burden of war from Englishmen's shoulders.

The dethronement of Richard II was a momentous decision. Despite the precedent of 1327, the situation in 1399 was different in one important respect. It was the first time since Richard the Lionheart's death that an English king had ended his reign without leaving a son and heir, and the realm now faced the possibility of a disputed succession. Custom since 1216 had vested the succession in the senior male line, even though that might mean a child-king (as in the case of Henry III and Richard II himself). But there was as yet no acknowledged rule of succession should the senior male line fail. In 1399 the choice by blood lay between the seven-year-old earl of March, descended through his grandmother from Edward III's second son, Lionel, and Henry Bolingbroke, the thirty-three-year-old son of King Edward's third son, John. Bolingbroke seized the Crown after being assured of support from the Percy family whom Richard had alienated. But in the extraordinary circumstances created by Richard II's dethronement and imprisonment, neither March nor Bolingbroke had obviously the stronger claim. No amount of distortion, concealment, and argument on Bolingbroke's part could disguise what was a *coup d'état*. Hence, as in the twelfth century, an element of dynastic instability was injected into English politics which contributed to domestic turmoil, and encouraged foreign intrigue and intervention in the following century.

England, meanwhile, could not escape the consequences of its earlier attempted subjugation of the 'Celtic' peoples in the British Isles. After the failure of Richard II's imaginative policies, a more stable relationship was needed to ensure security for the realm now that further conquest and colonization were patently beyond its resources. In practice, English kings abandoned all serious intention of implementing their claims to overlordship in Scotland and much of Ireland. In the fifteenth century, they were on the defensive against the Scots, partly because of the renewal of war in France and partly because of England's internal difficulties in Henry IV's reign (1399–1413) and after 1450; the Scots even sent substantial reinforcements to aid the French in 1419. For a brief time (1406–24), the captivity in England of King James I deterred major hostilities across the border, but thereafter the Scots became more daring, hoping to recover Roxburgh Castle and also Berwick, which they achieved in 1460–1. Raids, sea skirmishes, and piracy, together with ineffective truces, combined to produce a state of interminable 'cold war'. Only after the end of the Hundred Years War (1453) and the establishment of the Yorkist regime in England (1461) was there a really purposeful search for a more stable relationship. An Anglo-Scottish treaty was sealed in 1475, and a 'perpetual peace' in 1502, despite misgivings in France and the occasional English campaign in Scotland, such as Richard, duke of Gloucester's seizure of Berwick in 1482. This marked a significant shift in relations between the two countries, although border society continued to thrive on raids and disorder was a way of life.

The equilibrium reached in relations with Ireland was less satisfactory for England than for the Gaelic population and the Anglo-Irish nobility. Richard II's bold assertion of royal authority had failed, and was not repeated in the Middle Ages. The king's lordship of Ireland, though heavily subsidized from England, was consistently weak: the Gaels enjoyed independence and comparative prosperity, and the Anglo-Irish cherished their own power and came to terms with their Gaelic counterparts. The English government's main concern was security ('Ireland is a buttress and a post under England', declared a contemporary in the 1430s), and only when this was threatened during the Welsh rebellion (1400–9) and in the 1450s was more interest shown in Irish affairs. Internal political fragmentation and separation from England were the result. The greater Anglo-Irish magnates were the only source of power on which the government could rely to preserve some semblance of its authority: most Englishmen were reluctant even to go to

Ireland, effective rule from Dublin was impossible, and the resources for conquest simply did not exist. The real rulers of fifteenth-century Ireland were magnates such as the earls of Ormond and Kildare; even if the government had wanted to dislodge them, it could not. An equilibrium in Anglo-Irish relations was reached, but at the cost of surrendering effective English control.

In Wales, the heritage of complete conquest brought its own problems, notably a resentment which, in the unsettled economic climate of the late fourteenth century, was focused on the Anglicized boroughs and directed against officials in Church and State who were mostly from the English border shires or even further afield. This resentment was channelled into rebellion by Owain Glyndŵr from 1400, and after this unpleasant experience most Englishmen regarded Wales with suspicion and fear. One contemporary urged:

> Beware of Wales, Christ Jesus must us keep,
> That it make not our child's child to weep,
> Nor us also, if so it go this way
> By unwariness; since that many a day
> Men have been afraid of there rebellion....

Wales, then, posed a security problem and one much closer to hand. It not only provided a landfall for enemies from overseas (as at the height of Glyndŵr's rebellion and repeatedly during the Wars of the Roses), but was a land marred by misgovernment and disorder. Henry V showed firmness tempered by conciliation in dealing with Welshmen immediately after the rebellion collapsed, and marcher lords were ordered to attend to their lordships. But later on, neither the Crown nor the marcher lords were capable of sustaining vigorous rule, and the Welsh squirearchy, brothers-in-arms of the English gentry, showed less and less responsibility. Yet these Welsh squires were needed by the Crown and the marcher lords to govern Wales, for the Crown became immersed in civil war and by the fifteenth century the smaller number of lords were deterred from living in their lordships by falling incomes and Welsh hostility. The country, which by 1449 'daily abundeth and increaseth in misgovernance', consequently presented a problem of order—and therefore of security—for much of the century. Successive English regimes, from Henry VI to Henry VII, sought to keep the Welsh peaceful, improve the quality of government, and control the local squirearchy, for only then could the threat to the border shires and to the stability of the kingdom be lifted. In the first half of the century, the aim was to tighten up the existing machinery of law enforcement, relying on royal officers and marcher lords to fulfil their responsibilities. More radical and constructive solutions were eventually adopted, especially by Edward IV, who settled his son, the Prince of Wales, at Ludlow in the 1470s with a supervisory power in the principality of Wales, the marcher lordships, and the English border shires. This was a bold act of devolution that gave future princes responsibility throughout Wales.

The territorial power of the English magnates (the barons, viscounts, earls, marquesses, and dukes in ascending order of status) was crucial to the peace of the realm and the success of royal government. They became in the fifteenth century a strictly-defined and hereditary social group that was practically synonymous with the parliamentary peerage sitting in the House of Lords. The monarch could create peers (as Henry VI and Edward IV readily did) and could elevate existing ones to higher rank, while the king's patronage was essential to maintain magnate wealth and influence. Monarchs who did not appreciate this risked serious conflict with their magnates (as Richard II and Richard III discovered to their cost). Though few in number—at most sixty families, and perhaps half that figure after decades of civil war—they were vital not only because of the independent lordships which some of them held in the Welsh march and the dominance of the Nevilles and Percies in the north, but also because of their social and political control of the English provinces. They were a more effective buttress of the Crown than its own bureaucracy or civil service.

This was especially true in a century when three dynasties seized the Crown by force and had formidable military commitments at home and overseas to which the magnates made a notable contribution. The humiliation of defeat in France and the loss of English territories there was directly felt by the magnates and was something which Edward IV and Henry VII later strove to avoid.

These magnates had an identity of interest with the gentry of England—the 6,000 to 9,000 gentlemen, esquires, and knights who sought the 'good lordship' of the magnates and provided 'faithful service' in return. The magnates gave fees, land, and offices, and the gentry advice, support, and military aid: in 1454 the duke of Buckingham gave his badge to 2,000 of his retainers. Towns and townsmen were part of this relationship of mutual interest and service which historians have unflatteringly dubbed 'bastard feudalism'. The behaviour of the magnates and the gentry and townsmen in two distinct Houses of Parliament—the Lords and Commons—was another aspect of this interlocking relationship.

The co-operation of the magnates and their clients was especially vital to the usurping dynasties of the fifteenth century. The Lancastrians were well placed because Henry IV inherited the network of interests created by his father, John of Gaunt. At £12,000 a year, Gaunt was the richest magnate in late medieval England and his extensive estates and patronage were now at the disposal of his descendants as kings of England (1399–1461). The Yorkists (1461–85), as heirs of the earl of March, the alternative candidate in 1399, were less well endowed, except in the Welsh march. Their failure to enlist the support of most magnates was a serious weakness in a dynasty which survived for just twenty-four years. Henry VII, who inherited the estates, territorial influence, and patronage not only of Lancaster and York, but also of Neville, Beaufort, and other casualties of civil war, established the firmest control of all over the English magnates and gentry.

The first usurper, Henry IV, had the advantage of displacing a king who had alienated many and whose noble sympathizers were discredited. Henry's drive, perseverance, and powers of conciliation—not to say his generosity—and his Lancastrian connections enabled him to overcome the most daunting combination of enemies that any English king had faced. Richard II's die-hard supporters were foiled in their plot to assassinate Henry and his sons at Windsor Castle, and these rebels were apprehended and killed at Cirencester (December 1399). The danger from such 'Ricardians' led to Richard's own mysterious death in Pontefract Castle soon afterwards. The Percy earls of Northumberland and Worcester, virtual kingmakers in 1399, were so disenchanted by 1403 with the king's aim to win over all shades of opinion that they plotted several risings. Northumberland's son Hotspur, while marching to join the Welsh rebels, was defeated and killed near Shrewsbury. A Percy alliance with Archbishop Scrope of York raised the north of England, but Henry again acted quickly and in 1405 executed the prelate. Northumberland's last strike, with Scottish aid, collapsed at Bramham Moor, where the earl was slain (1408).

The Welsh rebellion had deeper roots in the soil of a colonial society. The distress experienced by a plague-ridden people, oppression by alien landowners bent on maintaining their incomes, a tendency to close the doors to opportunity against aspiring Welshmen, even resentment at Richard II's removal, combined to throw the country into revolt (1400). The variety of rebel motives and the divisions in Welsh society meant that this was no purely national, patriotic rising. Yet it was the most serious threat that Henry IV had to face and the most expensive to suppress. From his estates in north-east Wales, Owain Glyndŵr laid waste castles and Anglicized towns. He and his guerrilla forces exploited the mountainous terrain to harass and exhaust the enemy and then disappear 'among rocks and caves'. Their success can be measured by the length of the rebellion, the absence of decisive battles, and the fruitlessness of royal expeditions. Glyndŵr could occasionally muster 8,000 men, and he sought aid from France (1403) and fellow 'Celts' in

Scotland and Ireland (1401). In 'parliaments' in 1404 and 1405, he produced grand schemes for an independent Wales, with its own ecclesiastical organization and universities (aims which were not finally realized for another four centuries), and his alliance with the Percies was intended as a prelude to the dismemberment of Henry IV's realm.

The English, led by the king and his eldest son, Prince Henry, conducted several Welsh campaigns (1400–5), whose strategy was akin to that adopted in France—with pincer movements, destructive *chevauchées*, and co-ordinated supply by land and sea. The burden fell most heavily and frequently on the border shires and the West Midlands, which time and again were ordered to array men for service in Wales. These armies were substantial ones—4,000 strong—especially when one recalls that the armies sent to France rarely exceeded 5,000–6,000 men. But service in Wales was nothing like as popular as service in the lusher fields of France; there was difficulty in raising enough cash to pay the soldiers and garrisons, and in September 1403 Henry IV was told that 'you will not find a single gentleman who will stop in your said country'.

Generally secure in the north and west, Owain had his own problems of manpower, supply, and money, and the failure of his march on Worcester in 1405 caused his star to wane. He lost his Scottish ally when James I fell into English hands (1406), and an Anglo-French truce was arranged in 1407.

By 1408, the greatest dangers for Henry IV had passed: by perseverance, decisiveness, and a readiness to live in the saddle, as he pursued his enemies across England and Wales and to Edinburgh beyond, Henry overcame them all. By conciliation, he obtained Parliament's support without surrendering any significant part of his royal powers, and his four sons, Henry, Thomas, John, and Humphrey, were a maturing asset. Only two further threats to the dynasty occurred after his death in 1413. When the anticlericalism of certain courtiers turned to heresy the following year, Henry V did not hesitate to condemn even his old friend, Sir John Oldcastle. The last revolt before

1450 to be justified by the usurpation of 1399—that in favour of the earl of March in 1415—was suppressed just before King Hal left for France. Henry IV could claim considerable success in establishing his dynasty on firm foundations. International acceptance was won by alliances in Germany, Scandinavia, Brittany, and Burgundian Flanders.

Henry V inherited a realm that was sufficiently peaceful, loyal, and united for him to campaign extensively in France (from 1415) and to spend half of the next seven years abroad. With experience of war and government as Prince of Wales, he proved a capable, fearless, and authoritarian monarch who abandoned the careful ways of his father. Even during his absences in France, his kingship was firm and energetic, enabling him to wage a war that was as much a popular enterprise as Edward III's early campaigns had been. His reign was the climax of Lancastrian England.

Henry prepared for war by conciliating surviving Ricardians and renewing foreign alliances. The condition of France, with an insane king and quarrelsome nobles, encouraged his dreams of conquest. By 1415 he felt able to demand full sovereignty over territories beyond Edward III's vision and even to revive Edward's claim to the French Crown. Henry's ambitions coincided with his subjects' expectations. Large armies were raised under the leadership of enthusiastic magnates and knights; the realm voted taxation frequently and on a generous scale, and the king was able to explain his aims publicly so as to attract support. He even built a navy to dominate the Channel. This enthusiasm hardly faded at all before his death, though the parliamentary Commons expressed (1420) the same unease about the consequences for England of a final conquest of France as had their forebears to Edward III.

Henry V's strategy was Edward's—to ally with French nobles to exploit their divisions and press his own dynastic claim. Throughout the war, Burgundy's support was essential to English success. Quite soon, however, the invader's aims broadened into conquest and colonization on an unprecedented

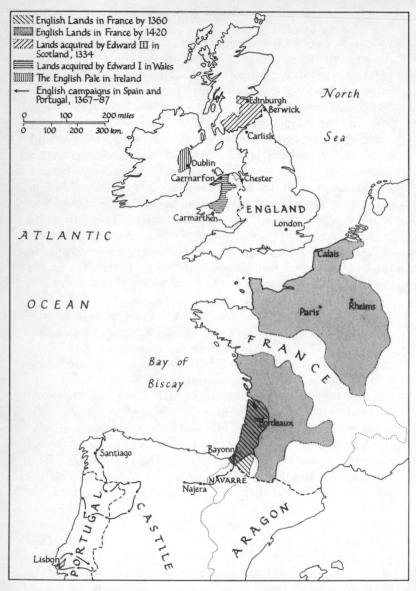

English Lands in France by 1360
English Lands in France by 1420
Lands acquired by Edward III in Scotland, 1334
Lands acquired by Edward I in Wales
The English Pale in Ireland
English campaigns in Spain and Portugal, 1367-87

0   100   200 miles
0   100   200   300 km

North

Sea

Edinburgh
Berwick

Carlisle

Dublin
Caernarfon
Chester

Carmarthen

ENGLAND

London

ATLANTIC

OCEAN

Calais

FRANCE

Paris
Rheims

Bay of

Biscay

Bordeaux

Bayonne

Santiago

NAVARRE

Najera

PORTUGAL

CASTILE

ARAGON

Lisbon

ENGLISH MILITARY ENTERPRISES IN WESTERN EUROPE IN
THE LATER MIDDLE AGES

scale. The 1415 expedition tested the water and the victory at Agincourt strikingly vindicated traditional English tactics. In 1417–20, therefore, Henry set about conquering Normandy which, along with adjacent provinces, was the main theatre of war during and after Henry's reign. The treaty of Troyes (1420) with Charles VI made him regent of France and heir to the Valois throne in place of the Dauphin. This extraordinary treaty dictated Anglo-French relations for more than a generation. Though Henry V never became king of France (he predeceased Charles VI in 1422), his baby son, Henry VI of England and, to the Anglophiles, Henry II of France, inherited the dual monarchy. It would require unremitting effort to maintain it.

Henry V and John, duke of Bedford, his brother and successor as military commander in France, pushed the Norman frontier east and south during 1417–29 and they defeated the French successively at Agincourt (1415), Cravant (1423), and Verneuil (1424). This was the high point of English power in France. Under Bedford, a 'constructive balance of firmness and conciliation' sought to make both the conquered lands and further campaigns (southwards in Anjou and Maine) pay for themselves. But the French resurgence inspired by Joan of Arc and the coronation of Charles VII at Rheims (1429) foiled this plan, and the English advance was halted after the defeat at Patay. Thereafter, the Normans grew restless under their foreign governors, England's Breton and Burgundian allies began to waver, and the English Parliament had to find yet more cash for the war in northern France where garrison and field armies were an increasingly heavy burden. The English were in a military as well as a financial trap—and without the genius of Henry V to direct them.

During the 1430s the search for peace became more urgent, particularly in England. The Congress of Arras (1435) and discussions at Gravelines (1439) were unproductive, largely because English opinion remained divided as to the desirability of peace and the wisdom of significant concessions. But the recovery in Charles VII's fortunes, the mounting cost of English expeditions to defend Lancastrian France, Bedford's death in 1435, and especially the defection of Burgundy were decisive factors. The government freed the duke of Orléans (a captive in England since Agincourt) to promote peace among his fellow French princes (1440), though he did not have much success. In 1445 Henry VI married the French queen's niece, Margaret of Anjou, but even that only produced a truce, and a proposed meeting of kings never took place. Eventually, Henry VI promised to surrender hard-won territory in the county of Maine as an earnest of his personal desire for peace. His failure to win the support of his subjects for this move—especially those magnates and gentry who had lands in France and had borne the brunt of the fighting—led to the exasperated French attacking Normandy in 1449. Their onslaught, supported by artillery, was so spectacularly successful that the English were defeated at Rouen and Formigny, and quickly cleared from the duchy by the end of August 1450. '... never had so great a country been conquered in so short a space of time, with such small loss to the populace and soldiery, and with so little killing of people or destruction and damage to the countryside,' reported a French chronicler.

Gascony, which had seen few major engagements under Henry V and Henry VI, was invaded by the triumphant French armies, and after their victory at Castillon on 17 July 1453, the English territories in the south-west were entirely lost. This was the most shattering blow of all: Gascony had been English since the twelfth century, and the long-established wine and cloth trades with southwest France were seriously disrupted. Of Henry V's 'empire', only Calais now remained. The defeated and disillusioned soldiers who returned to England regarded the discredited Lancastrian government as responsible for their plight and for the surrender of what Henry V had won. At home, Henry VI faced the consequences of defeat.

Within three weeks of Castillon, Henry VI suffered a mental and physical collapse which lasted for seventeen months and from which he may never have fully recovered. The loss of his

French kingdom (and Henry was the only English king to be crowned in France) may have been responsible for his breakdown, though by 1453 other aspects of his rule gave cause for grave concern. Those in whom Henry confided, notably the dukes of Suffolk (murdered 1450) and Somerset (killed in battle at St. Albans, 1455), proved unworthy of his trust and were widely hated. Those denied his favour—including Richard, duke of York and the Neville earls of Salisbury and Warwick—were bitter and resentful, and their efforts to improve their fortunes were blocked by the king and his court. Henry's government was close to bankruptcy, and its authority in the provinces and in Wales and Ireland was becoming paralysed. In the summer of 1450, there occurred the first popular revolt since 1381, led by the obscure but talented John Cade, who seized London for a few days and denounced the king's ministers. The king's personal responsibility for England's plight was inevitably great.

Henry VI was a well-intentioned man with laudable aspirations in education and religion; he sought peace with France and wished to reward his friends and servants. But no medieval king could rule by good intentions alone. Besides, Henry was extravagant, over-indulgent, and did not have the qualities of a shrewd and balanced judge of men and policies. He was intelligent and well educated, but he was the least experienced of kings and never shook off the youthful dependence on others which had been the inevitable hallmark of his long minority (1422–36). Many of his problems were admittedly unavoidable. The dual monarchy created by his father made heavier and more complex demands than those placed on a mainly military conqueror such as Edward III or Henry V. His minority was a period of magnate rule which created vested interests that were not easily surrendered when the king came of age—particularly by his uncle, Humphrey, duke of Gloucester, and his great-uncle, Henry Beaufort, cardinal-bishop of Winchester. Moreover, after Gloucester's death in 1447, Henry was the only surviving descendant of Henry IV in the senior male line, a fact which led him to distrust the duke of York, the heir of that earl of March who had been passed over in 1399. There was, then, ample reason for disenchantment with late Lancastrian rule, and in Richard of York there was a potential leader of the discontented.

Despite the king's illness, the birth of a son to his abrasive queen in October 1453 strengthened the Lancastrian dynasty, but it hardly improved the immediate prospect for the realm or for Richard of York. As England's premier duke and Henry's cousin, York was twice appointed protector of the realm during the king's incapacity (1454–5, 1455–6). But as such he aroused the queen's fierce hostility which erupted in the battles of Blore Heath and Ludford Bridge (September-October 1459), and in the subsequent Parliament at Coventry which victimized York, the Nevilles, and their supporters. This alienation of powerful men by a regime with a disastrous record at home and abroad led York to claim the Crown in October 1460. After his death at Wakefield soon after, his son Edward took it for himself on 4 March 1461, with the aid of the earl of Warwick. The period of dynastic war that is popularly known as the Wars of the Roses was now well under way amid conditions that had been ripening during the 1450s.

The new Yorkist monarch, Edward IV, suffered from a cardinal disadvantage: the deposed king, his queen, and his son were still at large. They thus provided a focus for their adherents and their Scots and French sympathizers, who were only too eager to embarrass a weak English regime. After Henry's capture in the north (1465), Edward felt more secure, though even then the former king was kept a prisoner in the Tower of London and his queen and son received shelter in Scotland and then in France. More serious still was Edward's failure to gain broad support from the English magnates and their clients. Furthermore, in the late 1460s he gradually alienated his powerful 'kingmaker', the earl of Warwick, who (like Northumberland after 1399) came to resent Edward's growing independence. Edward was also deserted by his feckless brother, George, duke of Clarence. These various elements combined to plot rebellion (1469) and, with encouragement from Louis XI of France, came to an uneasy agreement in July 1470 with the exiled Lancastrian Queen Margaret. Warwick, Clarence, Lancastrians, and dissident Yorkists returned to England and sent Edward IV fleeing to his ally, the duke of Burgundy. They promptly restored (or 'readepted') Henry VI, the first English king to have two separate reigns (1470–1). When Henry's Parliament assembled in November 1470, the chancellor was appealing beyond Westminster to the country at large when he took as the text of his opening sermon, 'Return O backsliding children, saith the Lord'.

But the deposed Edward, like Henry VI before him, was at liberty and he was able to raise a force with Burgundian help. Moreover, Henry's restored regime was undermined by a series of conflicting loyalties and mutually exclusive interests. Thus, when Edward returned to England in March 1471, he was able to defeat and kill Warwick at Barnet before marching west to vanquish at Tewkesbury the Lancastrian queen and prince, who had only just returned from France. At last Edward IV was dynastically secure: Queen Margaret was captured after Tewkesbury, her son was slain in the battle, and on the very night Edward returned triumphantly to London (21 May) Henry VI died in the Tower, most probably murdered. The main Lancastrian royal line was extinct. The Yorkist dissidents were either cowed or dead, and Clarence, though for a time reconciled with his brother, was subsequently executed for further indiscretions in 1478.

The relative political security which Edward enjoyed in the 1470s allowed him to attempt a period of constructive rule. He tried to repair England's reputation abroad by alliances with Brittany, Burgundy, and Scotland, and also by retracing the steps of previous kings to France. His expedition of 1475 was a near-disaster when his Breton and Burgundian allies proved fickle, but in the treaty of Picquigny Louis XI provided him with a handsome financial inducement to retire to England.

Edward's attempts to reorganize the government's financial administration were on lines suggested during the Lancastrian period. If he pleased Parliament by declaring his readiness to rule without special taxes, his desire to reward friends and attract political supporters meant that he could embark on no consistent programme of increasing his revenues. He curried favour with merchants and Londoners, participating in trade on his own account and maintaining good relations with Flanders and the Hanse League of German ports. Above all, the stability of his later years owed much to the continuity of service of several able and loyal officers of state.

Why, then, did the Wars of the Roses not come to an end and why did not posterity come to know of a Tudor dynasty only among the squirearchy of North Wales? The Yorkists fell victim in 1483–5 to two of the most common hazards to afflict a personal monarchy: a minority and a ruthlessly ambitious royal kinsman. When Edward IV died on 9 April 1483, his son and heir, Edward, was twelve. His minority need not have been long, and in any case England had weathered previous minorities without undue difficulty. But the degeneration of political behaviour since the 1450s, especially the often arbitrary, ruthless, and illegal actions of Edward IV, Warwick, and Clarence, made Edward V's accession particularly perilous. The Yorkist brothers, Edward, Clarence, and Gloucester, seem to have been unable to outgrow aristocratic attitudes to embrace the obligations of kingship in the short time their dynasty was on the throne. Edward relied on a circle of magnates, most of them linked with his own or his wife's Woodville family, to extend his authority in the kingdom: Gloucester in the north, the Woodvilles in Wales, and Lord Hastings in the Midlands. It worked well enough while Edward lived, but in 1483 the dangers of relying on an exclusive faction surfaced. Mistrust, particularly between Gloucester and the Woodvilles, undermined the ruling circle, and those outside it—not least the long-established Percies in the north and the duke of Buckingham in Wales and the West Midlands—saw their opportunity.

In these circumstances, the character and ambition of the sole remaining Yorkist brother, the thirty-year-old Richard of Gloucester, led him to contemplate seizing his young nephew's Crown for himself. He usurped the throne on 26 June, imprisoned (and probably murdered) Edward V and his brother, 'The Princes in the Tower', and executed the queen's brother and Lord Hastings. His only concession to customary rules of inheritance of the Crown was his unprincipled declaration that Edward IV and his sons were bastards; he ignored the children of Clarence. Richard III's actions and methods led to a revival of dynastic warfare. In October 1483, the duke of Buckingham, who was descended from Edward III's fifth son, Thomas, rebelled. More successful was the landing from France in August 1485 of Henry Tudor, though his claim to the throne through his mother, representing the illegitimate Beaufort line of Edward III's son, John, was tenuous. Nevertheless, at Bosworth Field on 22 August 1485 he vanquished and slew King Richard III. By then, Richard's own royal line seemed bankrupt: his wife and his only son were already dead.

A number of factors enabled Henry VII to keep his Crown after Bosworth. Alone among the usurpers of the fifteenth century, he was fortunate to have slain his childless predecessor in battle. The support which he received from the disillusioned Yorkists was crucial, especially that of Edward IV's queen. Also England's magnates were war-weary: their ranks were depleted, and in some cases their territorial power was either weakened or destroyed. As a result, attempts to dethrone Henry were poorly supported in England and the Yorkist pretenders (such as Lambert Simnel in 1487) failed to carry conviction. The actual fighting during 1455–85 may have amounted to only fifteen months, and the size of the armies involved may not have been very large; but the significance of a battle need bear no relation to the numbers engaged or the casualties sustained. The Wars of the Roses came close to destroying the hereditary basis of the English monarchy and Henry Tudor's seizure of the Crown hardly strengthened it. Henry posed as the representative and inheritor of both Lancaster and York, but in reality he became king, and determined to remain king, by his own efforts.

Towards a Nation

English kings enjoyed a mastery in their kingdom which French monarchs might have envied, and the Crown embodied the unity of England. Its wearer was not as other men. The coronation ceremony stressed his semi-spiritual quality, which seemed proven by the alleged power of the royal touch to cure the skin disease scrofula. Richard II insisted that those who approached him should bend the knee, and 'Majesty' became the common address in the fifteenth century.

The tentacles of royal administration—enabling decisions, grants of taxation, and legal pronouncements to be implemented—stretched to the extremities of the British Isles in every direction but the north and west. The franchises of the bishop of Durham and the earl of Chester stood outside the shire system of England and had a special independence. But there was no question of their being beyond the reach of the king's government: the bishops of Durham were almost always the king's choice and, like Anthony Bek (d. 1311) and Thomas Langley (d. 1437), often royal councillors; whilst after 1301 the earl of Chester was also Prince of Wales and the king's eldest son, and for most of the later Middle Ages the king administered Cheshire because there was no adult earl.

The king's administration was a co-operative affair. In each county the sheriffs and the newer justices of the peace functioned best with the aid of the nobility and local gentry, whose interests in turn were securely tied to the monarch, the greatest single source of wealth and patronage in the realm. Parliament, with its commons' representatives from counties and towns between Carlisle and Cornwall, Shrewsbury and Suffolk, came to play an essential part in late medieval government. By Edward I's reign, war and domestic upheaval had fortified the king's need to consult his subjects ('the community of the realm', as contemporaries termed them) and to seek their advice in reaching and implementing decisions affecting the realm at large. It also seemed wise, from time to time, to include local representatives as well as lay and ecclesiastical lords in a central assembly that was Parliament. The wish to tap the wealth of townsmen and smaller landowners as well as the nobility; the need for material aid and expressions of support in war and political crises; and the advisability of having the weight of a representative assembly behind controversial or novel changes in the law or in economic and social arrangements—all these factors combined to give Parliament a frequency (it met on average once a year during 1327–1437), distinctive functions, and established procedures, and to give the commons' representatives a permanent role in it from 1337 onwards. This institution, unique among the parliaments of medieval Europe, discussed both important matters of business and minor matters raised by individuals. It won a monopoly of taxing Englishmen; it was the highest court in the land; and it made new law and modified existing law through legislation. Even the commons' representatives won privileges for themselves, not least free speech and freedom from arrest during parliamentary sittings. It remained essentially an instrument of government at the king's disposal, but it could sometimes criticize his policies and ministers (as in the 1370s and 1380s and the 1440s), though almost never the king himself. When the practical needs that had brought Parliament into existence and encouraged its development disappeared, it met far less often: only once in every three years on average between 1453 (the end of the Hundred Years War) and 1509.

The commons' representatives had to be informed, courted, and persuaded before they returned home to their constituents, considerable numbers of whom desired information about affairs. It was, after all, they who paid taxes, served in war and defence, and who were asked for their co-operation and obedience. The government was, therefore, well advised to weigh carefully the news it transmitted to the realm and the opinions it hoped the king's subjects would adopt. Well-developed methods of communication and propaganda were used to this end. The preambles of official proclamations could popularize a policy and justify a practice: Edward IV's proclamation against Margaret, queen of the deposed Henry VI, made much of the memory of Archbishop Scrope of York, who had been executed by Henry's grandfather and had since taken on the aura of a martyr. This was skilful propaganda to sustain opposition to the Lancastrian dynasty, for proclamations were sent to every shire for public reading and display. Songs and ballads reached wide audiences too, and some that were officially inspired stressed the glories of Agincourt out of all proportion. Sermons were no less effective in moulding opinion and mobilizing support: in 1443 Henry VI requested that good, stirring preachers be sent through every diocese to reinforce from the pulpit royal appeals for money for yet another French campaign. Coronations, royal progresses, and the formal entries of kings and queens into York, Bristol, and Gloucester (as well as London) were occasions for lavish displays of official propaganda, harnessing mythology, Christianity, and patriotism. In 1417, Henry V was portrayed for all to see at his reception by London as a soldier of Christ returning from crusade against the French. If any citizen harboured lingering doubts about the justice of his invasion of France, this was calculated to remove them.

The circulation of letters to inform, persuade, and justify was as near as the pre-printing age came to publication; such letters soon found their way into popular chronicles. In this way, Henry V reported to his subjects the progress of his French campaigns. Even fashionable writers of the day became official propagandists. In the fifteenth century, authors rarely produced their works unsolicitedly. Thomas Hoccleve was a humble government bureaucrat who was paid by Henry V to produce laudatory verses about Agincourt and the English siege of Rouen (1419). John Lydgate was patronized by Henry VI and his court over a long period, implanting in the popular mind all the jingoism that could be wrung out of the successful defence of Calais against Burgundian attack in 1436.

The king, his court, and his ministers—the principal exploiters of these channels of communication—resided most often at Westminster, London, or Windsor. The shrine of English monarchy was Westminster Abbey, and Parliament usually met at Westminster (all thirty-one Parliaments did so between 1339 and 1371, and none met elsewhere after 1459). The departments of government gradually settled into permanent offices at Westminster or, to a lesser extent, London, which was the largest and wealthiest city in the land. In the later Middle Ages, it became the undisputed capital of the kingdom in every sphere except the ecclesiastical (where Canterbury remained the seat of the primate of All England). Along with Westminster and the growing riverside suburb in between, London became the administrative, commercial, cultural, and social focus for the kingdom. Government increased in extent, sophistication, and tempo in the later Middle Ages, particularly in wartime: regular taxes had to be collected and managed, frequent meetings of Parliament were held, the customs service was developed, the practicalities of war and defence had to be organized, and law and order throughout the kingdom was supervised there. Concentrated, co-ordinated, and sedentary government was the result. York lost its claims as a rival centre when the persistent war with Scotland in the first third of the fourteenth century was overtaken by the much greater preoccupation with France. Moreover, the absence of Edward III and Henry V on campaign abroad emphasized the trend towards a fixed, centralized governmental headquarters that could operate without the participation of the king himself. The crisis of 1339–41 brought home to Edward III that he could no longer take the machine of government with him, as Edward I and his predecessors had done. By 1340 the exchequer had returned to Westminster, which it never left again. The bureaucracy of the king's chancery, exchequer, and law courts expanded in the capital and, as a group of ambitious small landowners, in the neighbouring counties. Magnates, bishops, and abbots acquired inns or houses in or near the city, and the surnames of London's inhabitants and the language they spoke suggest that many humbler folk were migrating to the capital from every part of the kingdom—and from Wales and Ireland too.

The English character of the Church in England was its second most significant and enduring quality in the later Middle Ages. Its first was the Catholic faith and doctrine which it shared with other Latin churches. But it was widely accepted that this universal Church, headed by the pope in Rome as spiritual father, was a family of individual churches, each with its own character and autonomy. The Englishness of the Church in England became more pronounced in the later Middle Ages as the ecclesiastical dimension of English nationhood. This owed something to the English language and the separate experience of the English people, and a good deal to English law and custom, the framework within which Englishmen (including the clergy) lived and which the king swore to uphold in his coronation oath. Moreover, the Church of England, including its buildings, had been established, encouraged, and patronized by English kings, noblemen, gentry, and townsmen, giving them a personal and family interest in individual churches and their priests. The bishops were great landowners—the bishop of Winchester had an annual income of £3,900 in the mid-fifteenth century—who sat in Parliament and were among the king's councillors. They, and lesser dignitaries too, were usually promoted because they were trusted by, and useful to, the Crown and could be rewarded in the Church without cost to the exchequer. There were, then, good practical reasons why Englishmen should control the English Church and mould its character and personnel. This seemed the more urgent during the French wars. In 1307 and regularly thereafter, the pope's role in the organization and administration of the English Church, even in the appointment of bishops, was bitterly opposed. After all, most popes in the fourteenth century were French-born, and during 1308–78 they lived at Avignon, where they were in danger of becoming lap-dogs of the French (or so it was widely believed). By contrast, only one pope had been an Englishman (in the mid-twelfth century) and none had ever visited England—and would not do so until 1982.

The trend towards an Anglicized Church can be illustrated in several ways. Church law, based on the codes of the early Fathers and replenished by papal legislation, was received and generally applied in the Church courts of England, and the pope's ultimate jurisdiction in ecclesiastical matters was acknowledged. But in practice, Church law was limited by royal authority, particularly when clerks accused of crimes tried to claim 'benefit of clergy'. From Edward I's day, the pope's ability to tax the English clergy was severely curtailed and most papal taxes found their way into the king's coffers instead of fuelling the enemy's war effort (as many believed). More serious still were the limitations on the pope's power to appoint bishops and other important members of the English Church from the mid-fourteenth century onwards, and during the Great Schism (1378–1417, when there were two, sometimes three, popes simultaneously claiming Christendom's allegiance), the pope whom England supported was in no position to resist. The anti-papal statutes of Provisors (1351, reissued 1390) and *Praemunire* (1353, extended 1393) were used by English kings to impose a compromise on the pope whereby the initiative in appointments rested with the king. As a result, very few foreigners were appointed in the English Church by the fifteenth century unless, as with Henry VII's nomination of three Italian bishops, they had the government's specific approval.

Few clergymen in England protested at this state of affairs. The bishops did not do so because of the men they were and the way in which they were appointed. The Church did not do so corporately because it feared papal taxation. The clergy did not do so because English kings were the protectors of the faith against heretics and a buttress against anticlerical attack. In 1433, even an abbot of St. Albans could declare that 'the king knows no superior to himself within the realm'.

THE PRE-REFORMATION DIOCESES OF ENGLAND AND WALES
(THIRTEENTH CENTURY)

Predominantly English in character were two expressions of religious fervour outside the institutional church of late medieval England: the devotional fashion was strictly orthodox in theology, whereas the Lollard movement inspired by John Wycliffe was heretical. The fourteenth century saw a burgeoning interest in mystical and devotional writings, most of them in English from the latter part of the century and appealing to a growing literate public. Such people took for granted the teachings and practices of the Church but preferred a personal, intuitive devotion focused on the sufferings and death of Christ, the Virgin Mary, and the Lives of Saints, collected in the *Golden Legend*. The writers were frequently solitary figures commending the contemplative life to their readers. By far the most popular devotional works were by Richard Rolle, a Yorkshire hermit, and, later, by the recluse, Dame Juliane of Norwich. The *Book of Margery Kempe*, the spiritual autobiography of the wife of a Lynn burgess, exemplified the virtues which lay men and women sought, and the revelations, visions, and ecstasies by which they came to possess them. Laymen such as Henry, duke of Lancaster (who in 1354 wrote a devotional work of his own in French), and devout women such as Lady Margaret Beaufort, mother of Henry VII, turned to this intense spiritual life as a reaction to the arid theological discussions of scholars, though they did not stray into the unorthodoxy of Lollardy whose spiritual roots were not dissimilar.

Lollardy (probably a name derived from *lollaer*, a mumbler—of prayers) was the only significant heretical movement to sweep through medieval England, and Wycliffe was the only university intellectual in the history of medieval heresy to inspire a popular heretical movement against the Church. It was a largely indigenous English scheme of thought that laid great store by books and reading. Though Wycliffe is unlikely to have written in English, he inspired a series of English polemical works and also the first complete translation of the Bible by 1396. To begin with, he appealed to the anticlerical temper of his times and gained reputation and support among noblemen, courtiers, and scholars for his criticism of the Church's wealth and the unworthiness of too many of its clergy. But his increasingly radical theological ideas, placing overwhelming confidence in Holy Scripture, led to his condemnation and withdrawal from Oxford. The sympathy which he had received from influential men ebbed away when confronted with the strict orthodoxy of Henry IV (who added burning in 1401 to the armoury of the persecutors of heresy) and almost disappeared when Lollardy became tinged with rebellion in Sir John Oldcastle's rising. Deprived of its intellectual spring and its powerful protectors, Lollardy became a disjointed, unorganized but obstinate movement of craftsmen, artisans, and poor priests in the Welsh borderland and industrial towns of the Midlands. Their beliefs became more and more disparate and eccentric, but their basic hostility to ecclesiastical authority, their devotion to the Scriptures, and their belief in an English Bible prefigured the Reformation and were to be central convictions in later English Protestantism.

The spread of literacy and the increased use of the English language were twin developments of the late fourteenth and fifteenth centuries. They were symptomatic of Englishmen's growing awareness of public affairs, and reflect feelings of patriotism and nationhood.

It is easier to be persuaded of all this than to prove it in detail. There are no contemporary estimates of how rapidly and how far literacy spread; nor is it possible for us to quantify it with the data provided by largely innumerate contemporaries. A rough index of its growth becomes available if the statutes of 1351 and 1499 defining the legal privilege of 'benefit of clergy' (then the literate class) are compared. In 1351 it was stated that all laymen who could read should be accorded 'benefit of clergy'. One hundred and fifty years later, the situation had so changed that a distinction was drawn between mere lay scholars and clerks in holy orders, and only to the latter was 'benefit of clergy' now to be extended. Maybe the literate class had expanded to the point where 'clerical' was a meaningless adjective to apply to it, though the statute of 1499 attributed the need for change to abuse rather than to the expansion itself.

An equally generalized indication is provided by comparing the two popular risings of the later Middle Ages—the Peasants' Revolt (1381) and John Cade's rebellion (1450). In 1381 the complaints of the peasantry from Kent and Essex were (as far as we know) presented to Richard II orally, and all communications with the king during the revolt appear to have been by word of mouth; at the Tower of London, Richard had to ask that the rebels' grievances, hitherto roared at him by the insurgents outside, be put in writing for him to consider. Compare this with 1450, when the demands of Cade's followers, also drawn from Kent and the south-east, were submitted at the outset in written form of which several versions were produced and circulated. They are long documents, with a coherent and comprehensive argument, expressed in English, sometimes of a colloquial kind. The business of publishing manuscripts was extending its range at this very time. John Shirley (d. 1456) is known to have run his business from four rented shops near St. Paul's Cathedral and to have produced, for sale or loan, 'little ballads, complaints and roundels'. Twenty years later, customs accounts document the importation of large quantities of manuscript books through London—over 1,300 in 1480–1 alone.

One may cautiously introduce some figures to indicate that late medieval literacy was not confined to the noble, clerical, or governmental classes. As was probably the case with Cade's rebels, some artisans and craftsmen could now read and write. Eleven out of twenty-eight witnesses in a legal suit of 1373 described themselves as *literatus* (or capable of understanding Latin and therefore, one presumes, English too); and a mid-fifteenth century will provided a similar proportion of 'literates' among witnesses who included merchants, husbandmen, tailors, and mariners. There were doubtless others whom, literate or not, one would never dream of employing as witnesses, but we are undeniably moving towards Sir Thomas More's enthusiastic estimate at the beginning of the sixteenth century that more than 50 per cent of Englishmen were literate.

If we cannot accept such figures with complete confidence, we can at least observe literate men—rarely women—at work in a variety of occupations. They filled some of the highest political offices in the land hitherto reserved for clerics: from 1381, laymen frequently became Treasurer of England, an office for which a command of reading and writing—if not of figures—was an essential qualification. Literate laymen were employed as clerks in government service, a niche which the poet Thomas Hoccleve occupied for over thirty-five years. It is also clear that by 1380 tradesmen were keeping written bills; soon afterwards country yeomen were writing—certainly reading—private letters, and even peasants who served as reeve on their manor were functioning in an administrative environment whose business was increasingly transacted on paper and parchment. By Edward IV's time, the rules and regulations of some craft guilds were insisting on a recognized standard of literacy for their apprentices.

The reading habits of at least well-to-do laymen reflect the same thing. Reading chronicles was very popular, and not only in London; the surviving manuscripts alone run into hundreds and show signs of being produced in increasing numbers as the fifteenth century wore on—most of them in English. Merchants and others took to owning 'common-place books', those personal, diminutive libraries of poems, prophecies, chronicles, and even recipes, through which they browsed at leisure. They possessed books and carefully disposed of them—particularly the religious and devotional ones—in their wills.

This literate world was increasingly an English world. The facility to speak and understand French (and therefore to read and write it) was in marked decline before the end of the fourteenth century; even for official and formal business in government and private organizations, English was becoming at least as common. Discussions in Parliament were taking place in English by the middle decades of the century, and the first written record of this dates from 1362. Although only a rough and ready guide, it is worth noting that the earliest known property deed drawn up in English is dated 1376, the earliest will 1387. The proceedings of the convocation of Canterbury were conducted in English quite often by the 1370s, and Henry IV spoke to Parliament in English in 1399 and had his words carefully recorded. The reasons for this quiet revolution are complex, but among them may be numbered the patriotism generated by the long French war; the popularity of Lollardy, which set great store by English books and sermons; the lead given by the Crown and the nobility; and, of course, the greater participation of the English-speaking subject in the affairs of the realm, not least in Parliament. The triumph of the written language was assured.

Before that happened, one major problem had to be faced: that of regional dialects. Only then could the full potential of English as a written and spoken tongue be realized. It must be admitted that in this first century or so of popular, literate English, quaint Cornish, wilfully foreign Welsh, and such unintelligibilities as the Yorkshire dialect could not be fully absorbed into a common idiom; but much headway was made. The spreading tentacles of government helped, developing and extending the use of a written language for official communication throughout the realm during the first half of the fifteenth century. A further factor was the emergence in the fourteenth century of London as the settled capital of the kingdom, with York as a subsidiary administrative centre and Bristol as the second commercial metropolis, each evolving a dialect that inevitably became comprehensible to the others and gradually fused in a standardized English. This dialect was predominantly midland English, which triumphed at the expense of a city-bound tongue; and for this reason it was the more easily adopted in rural shires. That the victor was a midland dialect was in large part due to the substantial migration of midlanders and easterners to London in the fourteenth and fifteenth centuries. Lollardy was partly responsible too, for it was especially vigorous in the Midlands and West Country, and most of its written works were in varying forms of the midland tongue. By capturing London, this midland dialect in speech and writing captured the kingdom.

Geoffrey Chaucer had serious misgivings as to whether his writings would be understood across England—and he wrote for a limited, charmed circle.

> And for there is so great diversity
> In English and in writing of our tongue
> So pray I God that none miswrite thee,
> Nor thee mismetre for default of tongue.
> And read whereso thou be, or else sung
> That thou be understood, God I beseech.

In a legal case of 1426, it was stated that words were pronounced differently in different parts of England 'and one is just as good as the other'. Half a century later, William Caxton could be more optimistic that his printed editions of several hundreds would, with care, be quite comprehensible from one shire to another. He realized that 'common English that is spoken in one shire varieth from another'; but by using 'English not over rude, nor curious, but in such terms as shall be understood by God's grace', he anticipated little difficulty. The greater ease of understanding, in both speech and writing, that had developed meanwhile was crucial to the effectiveness of communication, the common expression of opinion, and the forging of a sense of nationhood.

English had become 'the language, not of a conquered, but of a conquering people'. The self-confidence of its writers reached the heights of genius in Chaucer, and it attracted patronage from the wealthiest and most influential in the realm—from kings, noblemen, gentlemen, and townsmen. English prose in the fourteenth and fifteenth centuries was far outshone in quality and popularity by English verse in all its forms: lyric and romance, comedy and tragedy, allegory and drama. Much of this poetry fell squarely in the northern European tradition, and the literary revival of the north-west and the Midlands in the fourteenth century was mainly of alliterative, unrhymed verse. But it was sponsored by local gentry and magnates such as the Bohuns (earls of Hereford) and the Mortimers (earls of March), and could produce works of considerable imaginative power in *Sir Gawain and the Green Knight* and *Piers Plowman*. In the same region, ritual Christian drama in the English Miracle Play Cycles was developed during the fourteenth century and achieved great popularity in northern towns such as York, Beverley, Wakefield, and Chester, where the plays were organized and performed by the town guilds.

At the same time, in the south and east, a newer mode of verse was appearing which owed more to current fashions of style and content in French and early Renaissance Italian writing. Through the pen of Chaucer, and to a lesser extent his friend John Gower, it created masterpieces of English literature. These were unequalled in their richness of thought and vocabulary, their imagination and depth of human understanding, and in their sheer artistry. *Troilus and Criseyde*, written about 1380–5, and especially the immensely ambitious and complex panorama of *The Canterbury Tales* (written 1386–1400 but never completed), decisively extended English literary accomplishment. They displayed a wisdom, worldliness, and inventiveness, and a mastery of contemporary English idiom in all its variety, which earn Chaucer his place as the greatest English medieval writer.

Gower, a Kentishman, was patronized by Richard II and, later, by Henry Bolingbroke. Chaucer, who came of London merchant stock, grew up in aristocratic and royal circles, and he was one of the most lionized and richly rewarded poets of any age. This reflects both the extraordinary quality of his writing, and also the recognition which influential contemporaries were prepared to give to the English language which he enriched. If Chaucer's disciples, Hoccleve and Lydgate, seem second-rate in comparison with their master, at least the royal, court, and city patronage which these authors received assured a bright future for what was essentially the English literary school of the capital.

The same sources of wealth and taste were placed at the disposal of England's architects and builders. Developing their ideas from the predominant Gothic style of much of Europe, of which the pointed arch is the symbol and most characteristic feature, they created architectural styles which have a good claim to be regarded as distinctively English. Since the nineteenth century, these have been termed Decorated (more accurately free-flowing and curvilinear) and Perpendicular (or rather vertical and rectilinear), and they are best identified in the window and arch design of England's cathedrals, larger parish churches, and colleges. In so far as any new architectural development can be explained with precision, it is thought that renewed diplomatic and crusader contacts with the Muslim and Mongol worlds of Egypt and Persia towards the end of the thirteenth century transmitted knowledge of Eastern building styles and techniques to the far West. The delicate tracery and luxuriant naturalistic motifs which are a feature of the new Decorated style appear on the three surviving Eleanor Crosses that Edward I erected in the 1290s to mark the stages in the journey of his wife's body from Lincoln to its burial at Westminster. Eastern influences have also been observed in the hexagonal north porch and doorway of St. Mary Redcliffe, Bristol, dating from early in the fourteenth century. After only half a century (1285–1335) of these extravagant complexities, which were unparalleled in Gothic Europe and have been hailed as 'the most brilliant display of sheer inventiveness in the whole history of English medieval architecture', a reaction set in. This reaction produced the most English style of all, the Perpendicular. In an age when England was at war, this was rarely imitated on the European mainland. Its simpler, cleaner lines and larger, lighter spaces may have appeared first in the royal chapel of St. Stephen, Westminster (destroyed 1834), or in the city cathedral of St. Paul (burned 1666). Either way, it quickly spread to the West Country, through courtly influence focused on Edward II's shrine at Gloucester. It can still be admired on the grand scale in the choir of Gloucester Cathedral, dating from the mid-1330s, as well as in the later naves of Canterbury (from 1379) and Winchester (from 1394). Decoration was now concentrated English-style in roof vaulting, culminating in the fan vaults of Hereford's chapter house (now destroyed) and the cloisters at Gloucester, which were built after 1351.

Yet Perpendicular building is found most frequently and at its best in the greater parish churches of England such as Cirencester, Coventry, and Hull. Not even plague and warfare, which may have inhibited large-scale projects for a while in the fifteenth century, could deter clothiers and landowners in East Anglia and the West Country from lavishing their wealth on these monuments to English taste and skill. Perpendicular architecture experienced an exuberant resurgence in the latter part of the fifteenth century in some of the most famous of English buildings, most of them sponsored by the Crown—Eton College, St. George's Chapel, Windsor (from 1474), King's College Chapel, Cambridge, and Henry VII's Chapel in Westminster Abbey. It was incontestably 'the Indian Summer of English medieval architecture'.

Incomparably English were the Perpendicular towers of late medieval parish churches, ranging from the sturdy St. Giles Church, Wrexham, to the soaring shaft of St. Botolph's, Boston, and the elegance of Taunton, St. Stephen's, Bristol, and St. John's, Cardiff. So, too, were the carved timber roofs of the fourteenth and fifteenth centuries, beginning with the timber vault planned for the chapter house at York after 1291, and the replacement of the tower of Ely Cathedral, which collapsed in 1322, by a timber vault and lantern tower. This roof work culminated in the great hammer-beam oak roof of Westminster Hall (1394–1400), commissioned by Richard II and judged to be 'the greatest single work of art of the whole of the European middle ages'. Masons, carpenters, and architects were patronized by kings, courtiers, noblemen, and others from the thirteenth century onwards, and not simply for religious building;

they also worked on royal and private castles and manor houses. Although forming a profession largely based in London and connected with the office of king's works, these craftsmen were assigned duties throughout England and Wales. They placed their expertise and experience at the disposal of noblemen and bishops and thereby created a national style to suit national tastes.

Englishmen's sense of nationhood and their awareness of their own Englishness are not easily gauged. But they sometimes compared themselves—and were compared by others—to peoples of different race, language, country, or cultural and political tradition. In the later Middle Ages, Englishmen confronted, frequently violently, other peoples both in the British Isles and in mainland Europe. These confrontations were a forcing-house of nationhood and self-conscious Englishness. Such experiences gave rise to a number of emotions, which made English people aware of their nature, unity, and common traditions and history.

So long as England was ruled by Norman dukes or Angevin counts, and Anglo-Norman barons held estates on both sides of the Channel and others did so in both England and Scotland, it was impossible for the ruling élite to think of itself as exclusively English. But this became possible once Normandy and Anjou were overrun by the French and formally surrendered to them in 1259, for the cross-Channel nobility had then to decide where its prime allegiance lay. It became more likely, too, with the growing self-consciousness of the Scottish kingdom, particularly when Edward I's wars made land-holding across the border a thing of the past. Thereafter, the separateness of England was identified with its encircling seas. In the mid-1430s a pamphleteer advised:

> Keep then the seas about in special;
> Which of England is the round wall,
> As though England were likened to a city
> And the wall environ were the sea...

English kings from Edward I were more truly English in upbringing and outlook than any since King Harold. Indeed,
Henry VI in his thirty-nine-year reign never visited Scotland or
Ireland; he only once set foot in Wales—a day at Monmouth—
and never again went to France after his coronation visit at the
age of nine.

As to foreigners, the dominance of Flemings and then Italians
in England's overseas trade in the thirteenth century fostered
resentment of their commercial success. In Henry VII's reign
Englishmen were said to 'have an antipathy to foreigners, and
imagine that they never come into their island but to make
themselves master of it and to usurp their goods...'. After all,
natives of a country at war with England might, like the alien
priories attached to French monasteries, send money to an
enemy, or, like the servants of Henry IV's queen, the duchess of
Brittany, act as spies for France. Not for nothing did the king's
clerks scratch 'Do not show to aliens!' on state papers at the
outset of the Hundred Years War.

England's wars, waged successfully by humble bowmen as
well as knights and noblemen, created among all ranks a self-
confidence that warmed English hearts. A well-informed observer said in 1373 that 'the English are so filled with their own
greatness and have won so many big victories that they have
come to believe they cannot lose. In battle, they are the most
confident nation in the world.' Pride in their victories seemed
unbounded, and individual kings embodied the achievements.
Under Edward III, 'the realm of England has been nobly
amended, honoured and enriched to a degree never seen in the
time of any other king', whilst Henry V's reputation among his
subjects reached even greater heights. Englishmen's belief in
their superiority—a short step from pride and self-confidence—
remained unshaken even in the mid-fifteenth century, by which
time England's fortunes seemed far less golden. The wild Gaels
were treated as 'mere Irish' and the Flemings in 1436 with
undisguised scorn:

Remember now, ye Flemings, upon your own shame;
When ye laid siege to Calais, ye were right still to blame;
For more of reputation, be Englishmen than ye,
And come of more gentle blood, of old antiquity.

An Italian visitor around 1500, when England's overseas 'empire' was all but lost, could still report that 'the English are great lovers of themselves and of everything belonging to them. They think that there are no other men than themselves, and no other world but England; and when they see a handsome foreigner they say that "he looks like an Englishman", and that "it is a great pity that he should not be an Englishman".' Feelings of superiority easily turned to disdain or even hate. After decades of war with the French, Francophobia was common and matched only by the Anglophobia of the French, who came to regard the English as 'a race of people accursed'. At no time was this distaste for things French stronger than during the reign of Henry V. He may have claimed the French crown, but in England he discouraged the use of the French language in government and literate society. The London brewers took their cue from their admired king, and when they wrote their ordinances in English they noted that 'our mother tongue, to wit, the English tongue, hath in modern days begun to be honourably enlarged and adorned ... and our most excellent lord, King Henry V, hath procured the common idiom ... to be commended by the exercise of writing'.

Tales of a British past and practical feelings of insecurity had combined with the vigour and ambition of English kings down to Edward I—perhaps Edward III—to take the English into Scotland, Wales, and Ireland. Their success in absorbing these territories was limited; and try as they might to Anglicize the Welsh and Irish in culture, language, and habit, the English with their dependent dominions were denied political nationhood in the later Middle Ages. The English delegation to the Church's Council at Constance (1414–17) declared:

whether a nation be understood as a people marked off from others by blood relationship and habit of unity, or by peculiarities of language (the most sure and positive sign and essence of a nation in divine and human law) ... or whether a nation be understood, as it should be, as a territory equal to that of the French nation, England is a real nation ...

But they spoilt their political case by adding that Scotland, Wales, and Ireland were part of the English nation.

FURTHER READING

1. THE EARLY MIDDLE AGES

GENERAL

M. T. Clanchy, *England and its Rulers 1066–1272* (Glasgow, 1983), a thought-provoking combination of political and cultural history.

G. W. S. Barrow, *Feudal Britain 1066–1314* (London, 1956), especially good on Scotland and Wales.

F. Barlow, *The Feudal Kingdom of England 1042–1216* (4th edn. London, 1988), an excellent outline.

D. M. Stenton, *English Society in the Early Middle Ages 1066–1307* (2nd edn. Harmondsworth, 1952), a brief social survey.

M. Chibnall, *Anglo-Norman England 1066–1166* (Oxford, 1986), judicious.

STUDIES OF SOME MAJOR POLITICAL THEMES

H. R. Loyn, *The Norman Conquest* (3rd edn. London, 1982), a brief and balanced survey of a standard problem.

J. Le Patourel, *The Norman Empire* (Oxford, 1976), magisterial. The starting-point for all future studies of this subject.

J. C. Holt, *Magna Carta* (Cambridge, 1965), indispensable for the political and social context of the charter.

G. O. Sayles, *The King's Parliament of England* (London, 1975), a distillation of 40 years of research and argument by Richardson and Sayles.

ROYAL BIOGRAPHIES

D. C. Douglas, *William the Conqueror* (London, 1964), a splendidly traditional biography.

F. Barlow, *William Rufus* (London, 1983), not just a life, also a fine study of the times.

R. H. C. Davis, *King Stephen* (London 1967), lively and stimulating. What could be better?

W. L. Warren, *Henry II* (London, 1973), somehow contrives to be both massive and readable.

J. Gillingham, *Richard the Lionheart* (2nd edn. London, 1989), emphasizes the importance of the Angevin dominions in France.

W. L. Warren, *King John* (Harmondsworth, 1961), seeks to rescue John from the damning verdict of thirteenth-century chroniclers.

OTHER BIOGRAPHIES

F. Barlow, *Thomas Becket* (London, 1986), a detached and detailed narrative.

C. R. Cheney, *Hubert Walter* (London, 1967), a lucid account of the career of the most powerful churchman of the age.

S. Painter, *William Marshal* (Baltimore, 1933), the story of a tournament knight who becomes regent of England.

CHURCH

F. Barlow, *The English Church 1066–1154* (London, 1979), a lively analysis of a radical and tumultuous age.

D. Knowles, *The Monastic Order in England 940–1216* (2nd edn. Cambridge, 1963), a scholarly history of monasticism by a scholar monk.

—— *The Religious Orders in England*, vol. 1 (Cambridge, 1962), important for the coming of the friars.

SCOTLAND

G. W. S. Barrow, *Kingship and Unity. Scotland 1000–1316* (London, 1981), an invaluable brief survey.

WALES

R. R. Davies, *Conquest, Coexistence and Change: Wales 1063–1415* (Oxford, 1987), economy, society, and politics: a major study.

IRELAND

R. Frame, *Colonial Ireland 1169–1369* (Dublin, 1981), an admirable sketch.

ECONOMY

J. L. Bolton, *The Medieval English Economy 1150–1500* (London, 1980), the most helpful general introduction.

E. Miller and J. Hatcher, *Medieval England: Rural Society and Eco-*

nomic Change 1086–1348 (London, 1978), a judicious survey of the rural economy.

S. Reynolds, *An Introduction to the History of English Medieval Towns* (2nd edn. Oxford, 1982), the thinking man's introduction to English urban history.

G. A. Williams, *Medieval London: from Commune to Capital* (London, 1963), a vivid and detailed account of thirteenth and early fourteenth-century London.

LANGUAGE AND LITERACY

M. T. Clanchy, *From Memory to Written Record: England 1066–1307* (London, 1979), a fascinating analysis of the development of literacy and the literate mentality.

ART

T. S. R. Boase, *English Art 1100–1216* (Oxford, 1953).

P. Brieger, *English Art 1216–1307* (Oxford, 1957): two classic surveys of art and architecture.

2. THE LATER MIDDLE AGES

GENERAL SURVEYS

F. R. H. DuBoulay, *An Age of Ambition* (London, 1970), a stimulating look at themes (e.g. class, marriage, sex) often neglected.

S. B. Chrimes, C. D. Ross, and R. A. Griffiths (eds.), *Fifteenth-century England, 1399–1509: Studies in Politics and Society* (Manchester, 1972), up-to-date essays on central topics.

J. R. Lander, *Conflict and Stability in Fifteenth-century England* (3rd edn. London, 1977), an overall (if gloomy) view of the century.

M. Prestwich, *The Three Edwards* (London, 1980), clear and succinct.

Anthony Tuck, *Crown and Nobility, 1272–1461* (London, 1985), a clear and sound narrative.

PARTICULAR THEMES

A. R. Bridbury, *Economic Growth: England in the Later Middle Ages* (London, 1962).

K. B. McFarlane, *The Nobility of Later Medieval England* (Oxford, 1973), essays by a master-historian.

R. H. Hilton, *The English Peasantry in the Later Middle Ages* (Oxford, 1975).

C. Platt, *The English Medieval Town* (London, 1976), a pleasant, illustrated book.

J. Bellamy, *Crime and Public Order in England in the Later Middle Ages* (London, 1973).

R. G. Davies and J. H. Denton (eds.), *The English Parliament in the Middle Ages* (Manchester, 1981), nicely integrated essays.

J. C. Dickinson, *An Ecclesiastical History of England: the Later Middle Ages* (London, 1979).

K. B. McFarlane, *John Wycliffe and the Beginnings of English Nonconformity* (London, 1952).

J. Evans, *English Art, 1307–1461* (Oxford, 1949).

V. J. Scattergood and J. W. Sherborne (eds.), *English Court Culture in the Later Middle Ages* (London, 1983), expert essays on a variety of themes.

S. Medcalf (ed.), *The Context of English Literature: The Later Middle Ages* (London, 1981), a rare attempt to integrate cultural and social history.

J. Brown (ed.), *Scottish Society in the Fifteenth Century* (London, 1977), essays on central topics.

Alexander Grant, *Independence and Nationhood: Scotland, 1306–1469* (London, 1984), a comprehensive and often original survey.

G. Williams, *Recovery, Orientation, and Reformation: Wales c.1415–1642* (*History of Wales*, vol. 3) (Oxford, 1987).

J. F. Lydon, *Ireland in the Later Middle Ages* (Dublin, 1973).

C. D. Ross, *The Wars of the Roses* (London, 1976), wise and well illustrated.

A. E. Goodman, *The Wars of the Roses* (London, 1981), good on military matters.

RECENT ROYAL AND POLITICAL STUDIES

E. L. G. Stones, *Edward I* (Oxford, 1978).

R. Barber, *Edward, Prince of Wales and Aquitaine* (London, 1978).

J. A. Tuck, *Richard II and the English Nobility* (London, 1973).

J. L. Kirby, *Henry IV of England* (London, 1970).

K. B. McFarlane, *Lancastrian Kings and Lollard Knights* (Oxford, 1972), two major themes explored with insight.

G. L. Harriss (ed.), *Henry V: The Practice of Kingship* (Oxford, 1985), essays which amount to a new study of the king and his reign.

R. A. Griffiths, *The Reign of King Henry VI* (London, 1981), more than a biography of the king.

C. D. Ross, *Edward IV* (London, 1974).

—— *Richard III* (London, 1981).

CHRONOLOGY

* Entries in *italics* denote events belonging to the history of the Roman Empire.

	Marcus Aurelius (161–80); major wars on the Danube
? c.163	Hadrian's Wall restored
193	Clodius Albinus proclaimed in Britain
	Severan Emperors (193–235)
196–213	Britain becomes two provinces
208–11	Campaigns of Septimius Severus and Caracalla in Scotland
235–70	*Imperial crisis: civil wars and invasions in East and West*
260–73	'Gallic Empire'
270s	Renewed growth in Britain
	Diocletian (284–305)
	'The Tetarchy'
287–96	Carausius and Allectus
296	Britain recovered by Constantius
after 296	Britain becomes a civil diocese of four provinces
	House of Constantius (305–63)
306	Campaign of Constantius I in Scotland; Constantine the Great proclaimed at York
324	*Constantine sole emperor; foundation of Constantinople*
340–69	Period of severe stress: internal troubles, harassment by barbarians
350	*Magnentius proclaimed in Gaul*
353	*Constantius II sole emperor*
353	Purge by Paul the Chain
	House of Valentinian (364–92)
367–9	'Barbarian Conspiracy', recovery and restoration of Britain by the elder Theodosius
	House of Theodosius (379–455)
	Theodosius the Great (379–95)
383	Magnus Maximus proclaimed in Britain; victory over Picts
	Honorius (395–423)
398–400	Victories over Picts, Scots, Saxons
400–2	Possible troop withdrawals by Stilicho
402/3	*Western imperial court withdrawn from Milan to Ravenna*
406	Britain revolts from Honorius: two emperors proclaimed

407	Constantine III proclaimed in Britain
	Constantine III rules from Arles (407–11)
409	Britain revolts from Constantine III: end of Roman rule in Britain
410	'Rescript of Honorius': letter to Britons (?), significance disputed
429	St. Germanus visits Britain
c.450	The *adventus Saxonum*: Hengest and Horsa settle in Kent (traditional date)
455	Hengest rebels against Vortigern (traditional date)
477	Saxon settlement of Sussex (traditional date)
495	Saxon settlement of Wessex (traditional date)
c.500	Battle of *Mons Badonicus*
560	Æthelberht, later over-king, becomes king in Kent
577	The West Saxons capture Gloucester, Cirencester and Bath
597	St. Augustine's mission arrives in Kent
616	Raedwald of East Anglia, as over-king, makes Edwin king of Northumbria
c.624	Death of Raedwald, and his probable burial in the Sutton Hoo barrow
627	Conversion of Edwin and the Northumbrian court
633	Battle of Heavenfield; Oswald of Northumbria becomes over-king
635	Conversion of King Cynegils of Wessex
642	Oswald is killed at Oswestry by King Penda of Mercia
655	Penda is defeated and killed at the *Winwaed* by Oswy of Northumbria, who becomes over-king
664	Synod of Whitby
669	Arrival of Archbishop Theodore
672	Synod of Hertford; battle of the Trent, marking the beginnings of the rise of Mercia
685–8	Expansion of Wessex under Caedwalla to include Kent, Surrey and Sussex
716	Æthelbald become king of Mercia
731	Bede completes his *Ecclesiastical History*
746–7	First Council of Clofesho
757	Death of Æthelbald; Offa becomes king of Mercia
786	Legatine Council held under Offa

793–5	Danish raids on Lindisfarne, Jarrow, and Iona
796	Death of Offa
825	Egbert of Wessex defeats Mercia and annexes Kent, Essex, Surrey, and Sussex
835	Big Danish raid on Kent
865	The Danish 'Great Army' lands
867	Northumbria falls to the Danes
870	East Anglia falls to the Danes; murder of St. Edmund
871	The Danes attack Wessex; Alfred becomes king
874	Mercia falls to the Danes
878	(March) The Danes drive Alfred into the Somerset marshes
	(May) Alfred defeats the Danes at Edington; Guthrum is baptized
899	Death of Alfred; Edward 'the Elder' becomes king of Wessex
910–20	Edward and Æthelflaed reconquer most of the Danelaw
919	Norse kingdom of York is founded by Raegnald
924	Death of Edward; Athelstan becomes king
937	Athelstan defeats the Norse, Scots and Strathclyde Welsh at Brunanburh
939	Death of Athelstan; Edmund become king
940	Dunstan begin to refound Glastonbury as a regular monastic house
946	Death of Edmund
954	The last king of York is deposed
959	Edgar becomes king
960	Dunstan becomes Archbishop of Canterbury
c.970	*Regularis Concordia* is compiled
973	Edgar is crowned and consecrated, and receives the submission of British princes
975	Death of Edgar; Edward 'the Martyr' becomes king
979	Murder of Edward; Æthelred 'the Unready' becomes king
991	The Danes defeat Alderman Byrhtnoth and the Essex levies at Maldon; treaty between England and Normandy
1002	Æthelred orders the massacre of all Danes in England

1003	Danish invasion led by King Swein
1013	Swein returns with a new army; the Danelaw accepts him as king
1014	Swein dies; the Danish army in England elect Cnut as their king
1016	(April) Æthelred dies; Edmund 'Ironside' becomes king
	(autumn) Cnut defeats Edmund at Ashingdon; Edmund dies and Cnut becomes King of all England
1017	Cnut divides England into four earldoms
1035	Death of Cnut
1037	Harold becomes king
1040	Death of Harold; Harthacnut becomes king
1042	Death of Harthacnut; Edward 'the Confessor' becomes king
1051–2	Conflict between King Edward and Godwin earl of Wessex
1053	Death of Godwin; his son Harold becomes earl of Wessex
1064–5	Earl Harold visits Duke William in Normandy
1066	(January) Death of King Edward; Earl Harold becomes king
	(September) King Harold of England defeats and kills King Harold of Norway at Stamford Bridge
	(October) Duke William of Normandy defeats and kills King Harold of England at Hastings

VOL. 2 THE MIDDLE AGES

1066	(December) William is consecrated king
1067–70	English rebellions
1069–70	The harrying of the north
1086	Domesday Survey carried out
1087	Death of William I; accession of William II Rufus
1088	Rebellion in support of Robert Curthose
1093	Anselm appointed Archbishop of Canterbury
1096	Robert pawns Normandy ot Rufus
1100	Death of William Rufus; accession of Henry I
1101	Invasion of Robert Curthose
1106	Battle of Tinchebray; Curthose imprisoned; Henry I takes Normandy
1107	Settlement of Investiture Dispute in England

1120	Wreck of the White Ship
1128	Marriage of Empress Matilda to Geoffrey of Anjou
1135	Death of Henry I; accession of Stephen
1139–53	Civil war in England
1141	Battle of Lincoln; Stephen captured; later exchanged for Robert of Gloucester
1141–5	Geoffrey of Anjou conquers Normandy
1149	Cession of Northumbria to David of Scotland
1152	Henry of Anjou (later Henry II) marries Eleanor of Aquitaine
1153	Henry invades England; he and Stephen come to terms
1154	Death of Stephen; accession of Henry II
1157	Henry regains Northumbria
1162	Becket appointed Archbishop of Canterbury
1164	Council and Constitutions of Clarendon; Becket goes into exile
1166	Assize of Clarendon
1169–72	English conquest of Ireland begins
1170	Coronation of the young king; murder of Becket
1173–4	Rebellion against Henry II; William 'the Lion' (king of Scotland) invades the north
1183	Death of the young king
1189	Death of Henry II; accession of Richard I
1190–92	Richard I on crusade
1193–4	Richard in prison in Germany
1193–1205	Hubert Walter, Archbishop of Canterbury (justiciar 1194–8; chancellor 1199–1205)
1197	Death of Rhys of Deheubarth
1199	Death of Richard I; accession of John; establishment of Chancery Rolls
1203–4	Philip Augustus conquers Anjou and Normandy
1208–14	Interdict in England
1214	Battle of Bouvines: French victory
1215	Magna Carta; civil war in England
1216	Louis (later Louis VIII) invades; death of John; accession of Henry III
1217	Battles of Lincoln and Dover; Louis withdraws
1221–4	Arrival of Dominican and Franciscan Friars in England
1224	Louis VIII completes conquest of Poitou

1232	Dismissal of Hubert de Burgh
1240	Death of Llywelyn the Great
1254	Henry III accepts papal offer of throne of Sicily
1258	Barons take over royal government; provisions of Oxford
1259	Treaty of Paris between England and France
1264	Battle of Lewes; Henry III captured; government of Simon de Montfort
1265	Battle of Evesham; killing of Simon de Montfort
1267	Henry recognizes Llywelyn ap Gruffydd as Prince of Wales
1272	Death of Henry III; accession of Edward I
1276–7	First Welsh War
1282–3	Edward's conquest of Wales
1286–9	Edward I in Gascony
1291	Edward I asserts his overlordship over Scotland
1294	War with France begins
1295	Franco-Scottish alliance
1296	Edward I invades Scotland; his conflict with the Church
1297	Edward I's conflict with his magnates; his expedition to Flanders
1306	Rebellion of Robert Bruce
1307	Death of Edward I; accession of Edward II
1314	Scottish victory at Bannockburn
1315–16	Great famine
1321–2	Civil war in England
1327	Deposition and death of Edward II; accession of Edward III
1330	Edward III takes the reins of government
1337	The Hundred Years War begins
1339–41	Political crisis in England
1346	English victories at Crécy and Neville's Cross
1347	English capture Calais
1348	First occurrence of plague in England
1356	English victory at Poitiers
1361	Second major occurrence of plague
1376	'Good Parliament' meets; death of Edward, the Black Prince
1377	Death of Edward III; accession of Richard II

1622–3	Prince Charles and Buckingham go to Spain to woo the king's daughter and are rebuffed
1624–30	War with Spain
1625	Death of James I; accession of Charles I and marriage to Henrietta Maria, sister of Louis XIII of France
1626–9	War with France
1628	Petition of Right; publication of Harvey's work on the circulation of the blood; assassination of Buckingham
1629	Charles I dissolves Parliament, determines to govern without one
1630	Large-scale emigration to Massachusetts begins
1633	William Laud translated to be Archbishop of Canterbury
1634–40	Ship Money case
1637	Hampden's case supports Charles I's claim to collect Ship Money
1637–40	Breakdown of Charles's government of Scotland and two attempts to impose his will by force
1640	Long Parliament summoned
1641	Remodelling of government in England and Scotland; abolition of conciliar courts, abolition of prerogative taxation, triennial bill, Grand Remonstrance; rebellion of Ulster Catholics
1642	King's attempt on the Five Members; his withdrawal from London; the 19 Propositions; the resort of arms: Civil War
1643	King's armies prosper; Scots invade on side of Parliament
1644	Parliamentary armies prosper, especially in the decisive battle of the war, Marston Moor (June)
1645	'Clubmen' risings of armed neutrals threaten both sides; Royalist armies disintegrate, but parliamentary forces reorganized (New Model Army)
1646	King surrenders to the Scots; bishops and Book of Common Prayer abolished, Presbyterian Church established
1647	Army revolt; radical movements criticize parliamentary tyranny; king prevaricates

1648	Second Civil War: Scots now side with the king and are defeated; provincial risings (Kent, Colchester, South Wales, Yorks., etc.) crushed
1649	Trial and execution of Charles I: England a Republic
1649–53	Government by sovereign single-chamber assembly, the 'Rump' Parliament thoroughly purged of royalists and moderates
1649–50	Oliver Cromwell conquers Ireland (Drogheda massacre)
1650–2	Oliver Cromwell conquers Scotland (battles of Dunbar and Worcester)
1651	Thomas Hobbes's *Leviathan* published
1652–4	First Dutch War
1653	Cromwell dissolves Rump, creates the Nominated or Barebones Assembly; it surrenders power back to him, and he becomes Lord Protector under a paper constitution (*The Instrument of Government*)
1655–60	War with Spain
1655	Royalist insurrection (Penruddock's rising) is a complete failure
1657	*Instrument of Government* replaced by a parliamentary paper constitution, the *Humble Petition and Advice*; Cromwell rejects title of King and remains Lord Protector, but nominates his own House of Lords
1658	Cromwell dies and is succeeded by his son Richard
1659	Richard overthrown by the army; Rump restored but displeases many in the army
1660	Charles II restored
1662	Church of England restored; Royal Society receives its Charter
1663	Failure of first royal attempt to grant religious toleration
1665–7	Second Dutch War
1665	Great Plague (final major outbreak)
1666	Great Fire of London
1667	Milton's *Paradise Lost* published
1672–3	Failure of second royal attempt to grant religious toleration
1672–4	Third Dutch War

1674	Grain bounties introduced (England self-sufficient in food)
1678	Titus Oates and the Popish Plot; Bunyan's *Pilgrim's Progress*, part I, published
1679–81	The Exclusion Crisis; emergence of Whig and Tory parties
1683	The Rye House Plot; Whigs proscribed
1685	Charles II dies; accession of James II; rebellion by Charles II's protestant bastard, the duke of Monmouth, fails
1687	James II's Declaration of Indulgence; Tories proscribed; Newton's *Principia Mathematica* published
1688	James II's son born
1688	William of Orange invades: James II takes flight, accession of William III (of Orange) and Mary

VOL. 4 THE EIGHTEENTH AND EARLY NINETEENTH CENTURIES

1689	Bill of Rights settles succession to the throne and declares illegal various grievances; Toleration Act grants rights to Trinitarian Protestant dissenters
1690	Battle of the Boyne: William III defeats Irish and French army
1694	Bank of England founded; death of Queen Mary; Triennial Act sets the maximum duration of a parliament at three years
1695	Lapse of Licensing Act
1697	Peace treaty of Ryswick between allied powers of the League of Augsburg and France; Civil List Act votes funds for the maintenance of the royal household
1701	War of Spanish Succession begins; Act of Settlement settles the royal succession on the descendants of Sophia of Hanover
1702	Death of William III; accession of Anne
1704	Battle of Blenheim: British, Dutch, German and Austrian troops defeat French and Bavarian forces; British capture of Gibraltar from Spain
1707	Union of England and Scotland
1710	Impeachment of Dr Sacheverell; Harley ministry
1713	Peace treaty of Utrecht concludes the War of Spanish Succession

1714	Death of Anne; accession of George I
1715	Jacobite rebellion aimed at overthrowing the Hanoverian succession fails
1716	Septennial Act sets the maximum duration of a parliament at seven years
1717	Whig split; suspension of convocation
1720	South Sea Bubble: many investors ruined after speculation in the stock of the South Sea Company
1721	Walpole ministry
1722	Atterbury Plot, the most notable Jacobite plot
1726	Jonathan Swift's *Gulliver's Travels* published
1727	Death of George I; accession of George II
1729	Alexander Pope's *Dunciad* published
1730	Walpole/Townshend split
1733	Excise crisis: Walpole has to abandon his plans to reorganize the customs and excise
1737	Death of Queen Caroline
1738	Wesley's 'conversion': the start of Methodism
1739	War of Jenkins' Ear: Anglo-Spanish naval war
1740	War of the Austrian Succession
1741	Samuel Richardson's *Pamela* published
1742	Fall of Walpole
1744	Ministry of Pelham
1745	Jacobite Rebellion led by 'Bonnie Prince Charlie'
1746	Battle of Culloden: the duke of Cumberland routs the Jacobite army
1748	Peace of Aix-la-Chapelle concludes War of the Austrian Succession
1752	Adoption of Gregorian Calendar
1753	Jewish Naturalization Bill
1754	Newcastle ministry
1756	Seven Years War: Britain allied with Frederick the Great of Prussian against France, Austria, and Russia
1757	Pitt–Newcastle ministry; battle of Plassey: British victory over Bengal
1759	Capture of Quebec: British victory over the French
1760	Death of George II; accession of George III
1761	Laurence Sterne's *Tristram Shandy* published
1762	Bute's ministry
1763	Peace of Paris concludes Seven Years War; Grenville

1796   Vaccination against smallpox introduced
1798   T. R. Malthus's *Essay on Population* published; tax of
           ten per cent on incomes over £200 introduced
1799   Trade Unions suppressed; Napoleon appointed First
           Consul in France
1799–1801 Commercial boom
1801   Union with Ireland; first British Census
1802   Peace with France; Peel introduces first factory
           legislation
1803   War with France; General Enclosure Act simplifies
           process of enclosure of common land
1805   Battle of Trafalgar: Nelson defeats the French and
           Spanish fleets
1809–10   Commercial boom
1811   Depression because of Orders in Council; 'Luddite'
           disturbances in Nottinghamshire and Yorkshire;
           George, Prince of Wales, made Prince Regent
1813   East India Company's monopoly abolished
1815   Battle of Waterloo: defeat of Napoleon; peace in
           Europe: Congress of Vienna; Corn Law passed
           setting price of corn at 80s. per quarter
1815–17   Commercial boom
1817   Slump; the Blanketeers' march and other disturbances
1819   Peterloo massacre: troops intervene at mass reform
           meeting, killing 11 and wounding 400
1820   Death of George III; accession of George IV
1821–3   Famine in Ireland
1824   Commercial boom
1825   Trade Unions legalized; Stockton and Darlington
           railway opens; commercial depression
1829   Catholic Emancipation, ending most denials or
           restrictions of Catholic civil rights, ownership of
           property, and holding of public office
1830   Death of George IV; accession of William IV;
           Liverpool and Manchester railway opens
1830–2   First major cholera epidemic; Whigs in power under
           Grey
1831   'Swing' riots in rural areas against the mechanization
           of agriculture
1832   Great Reform Bill brings climax to period of political

1882	Britain occupies Egypt; Triple Alliance between Germany, Austria, and Italy
1884–5	Reform and Redistribution Acts
1885	Death of Gordon at Khartoum; Burma annexed; Salisbury's first (minority) Conservative government
1886	Royal Niger Company chartered; gold found in Transvaal; Gladstone's third Liberal government introduces first Home Rule Bill for Ireland: Liberal Party splits
1886–92	Salisbury's second (Conservative–Liberal-Unionist) government
1887	British East Africa Company chartered
1888	County Councils Act establishes representative county authorities
1889	London dock strike; British South Africa Company chartered
1892–4	Gladstone's fourth (minority) Liberal government
1893	Second Home Rule Bill rejected by the Lords; Independent Labour Party founded
1894–5	Rosebery's minority Liberal government
1895–1902	Salisbury's third Unionist ministry
1896–8	Sudan conquered
1898	German naval expansion begins
1899–1902	Second Anglo-Boer War
1899	(autumn)British disasters in South Africa
1900	Khaki election won by Salisbury; formation of Labour Representation Committee; Commonwealth of Australia Act
1901	Death of Victoria; accession of Edward VII
1902	Balfour's Education Act; Anglo-Japanese alliance
1902–5	Balfour's Unionist government
1903	Chamberlain's Tariff Reform campaign starts
1904	Anglo-French *Entente*
1905–8	Campbell-Bannerman's Liberal government
1906	Liberals win general election (January); Labour Party formed
1907	Anglo-Russian *Entente*
1908–15	Asquith's Liberal government
1908	Asquith's Old Age Pensions plan introduced

1909	Churchill's Employment Exchanges introduced; Lloyd George's budget rejected by Lords; Union of South Africa Act
1910	(January) General election: Liberal government retains office
	(May) Death of Edward VII; accession of George V
	(December) General election: Liberal government again retains office
1911	Parliament Act curtails power of the House of Lords, establishes five-yearly elections; Lloyd George's National Insurance Act; Moroccan crisis
1911-12	Railway, mining, and coal strikes
1912	Anglo-German navy talks fail
1912-14	Third Home Rule Act (for Ireland) and Welsh Church Disestablishment Act passed, but suspended
1914	(28 June) Assassination of Archduke Ferdinand at Sarajevo
	(4 August) British Empire enters the First World War
1915-16	Dardanelles expedition, ending in British withdrawal from Gallipoli
1916	Battle of the Somme; battle of Jutland; Lloyd George succeeds Asquith as Prime Minister
1917	Battle of Passchendaele
1918	End of First World War (11 November); Lloyd George coalition government returned in 'coupon election' (December)
1919	Treaty of Versailles establishes peace in Europe
1921	Miners seek support of dockers' and railwaymen's unions (the 'Triple Alliance') in major strike: on 'Black Friday' the dockers and railwaymen back down, and the alliance is broken; Lloyd George concludes treaty with Sinn Fein
1922	Fall of Lloyd George; Bonar Law heads Conservative government
1923	Baldwin becomes Conservative Prime Minister; general election
1924	(January) MacDonald leads first Labour government
	(November) Conservatives return to office under Baldwin

1925	Britain goes back on the gold standard
1926	General Strike (3–12 May)
1929	General election; MacDonald leads second Labour government
1931	Financial crisis and run on the pound; Britain abandons the gold standard; MacDonald resigns and is returned in the election to head National government
1932	Ottawa Conference on imperial trade institutes protective tarriffs
1935	Conservatives win general election: Baldwin succeeds MacDonald as Prime Minister; Hoare–Laval pact on Abyssinia; Government of India Act
1936	Death of King George V; abdication of Edward VIII: George VI becomes king
1937	Neville Chamberlain succeeds Baldwin as Conservative Prime Minister
1938	Chamberlain meets Hitler at Berchtesgaden, Godesberg, and Munich
1939	British guarantee to Poland; British Empire declares war on Germany (3 September)
1940	Churchill succeeds Chamberlain as Prime Minister; withdrawal from Dunkirk; Battle of Britain
1941	*Luftwaffe* 'blitz' on many British cities; Soviet Union and United States enter the war
1942	Loss of Singapore; Montgomery's victory at El Alamein; battle of Stalingrad; Beveridge Report on social security
1943	Successful campaign in North Africa; Anglo-American armies invade Italy
1944	D-day invasion of France; Butler's Education Act
1945	End of war in Europe (8 May) and in far East (15 August); general election: massive Labour victory and Attlee becomes Prime Minister
1947	Coal and other industries nationalized; convertibility crisis; transfer of power to independent India, Pakistan, and Burma
1949	NATO founded; devaluation of the pound by Cripps
1950	General election: Labour retains power by narrow

majority; outbreak of war in Korea

1951 Festival of Britain; general election: Conservatives defeat Labour, and Churchill again becomes Prime Minister

1952 Death of King George VI; Queen Elizabeth II proclaimed

1954 British troops withdraw from Egypt

1955 Eden becomes Prime Minister; general election won by Conservatives

1956 Anglo-French invasion of Suez, followed by withdrawal

1957 Eden resigns; Macmillan becomes Prime Minister

1959 General election: Conservatives win with larger majority

1963 French veto Britain's application to join the European Common Market; test-ban treaty in Moscow limits nuclear testing; Douglas-Home succeeds Macmillan as Prime Minister

1964 General election: Labour under Harold Wilson win narrow majority

1966 General election: Labour win with much larger majority

1967 Devaluation of the pound

1970 General election: Conservatives under Edward Heath returned to office

1972 National miners' strike; Stormont government abolished in Northern Ireland

1973 Britain enters European Common Market

1974 National miners' strike; two general elections: Labour under Harold Wilson win both with narrow majorities

1975 Popular referendum confirms British membership of the Common Market

1976 Economic crisis: Britain obtains help from International Monetary Fund

1979 Devolution referendums in Wales and Scotland; general election: Conservatives under Mrs Thatcher returned to office; independence granted to Zimbabwe (Rhodesia)

1980 Britain becomes self-sufficient in North Sea oil

1981   Social Democratic Party founded

1982   Britain defeats Argentina in war over the Falkland Islands

1983   General election: Mrs Thatcher's Conservative government returned with massive majority; Cruise missiles installed

1984   Miners' strike

1985   Miners' strike ends after a year; Anglo-Irish Hillsborough Agreement signed

1986   Channel Tunnel treaty signed; 'Big Bang' in Stock Exchange

1987   General election: Mrs Thatcher's Conservative government again returned with a majority of over 100; Stock Exchange collapse in the autumn

NORMAN AND PLANTAGENET
1066–1327

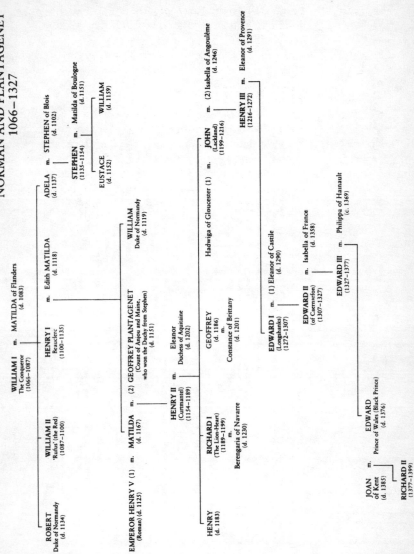

LANCASTER AND YORK
1327–1485

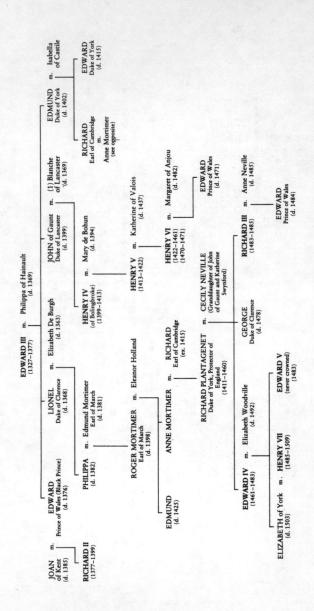